EXECUTIVE EDITOR
Natalie Earnheart

CREATIVE TEAM
Jenny Doan, Natalie Earnheart, Christine Ricks,
Tyler MacBeth, Mike Brunner, Lauren Dorton,
Jennifer Dowling, Dustin Weant, Jessica Toye,
Kimberly Forman, Denise Lane

EDITORS & COPYWRITERS
Nichole Spravzoff, Camille Maddox,
David Litherland, Julie Barber-Arutyunyan

SEWIST TEAM
Jenny Doan, Natalie Earnheart, Carol Henderson,
Janice Richardson, Aislinn Earnheart

PRINTING COORDINATOR
Rob Stoebener

PRINTING SERVICES
Walsworth Print Group
803 South Missouri
Marceline, MO 64658

CONTACT US
Missouri Star Quilt Company
114 N Davis
Hamilton, MO 64644
888-571-1122
info@missouriquiltco.com

contents

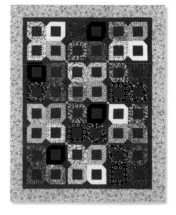
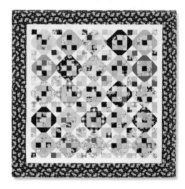

Oops! Sometimes we make mistakes. To find corrections to every issue of BLOCK go to: **www.msqc.co/corrections**

3

A note from Jenny

Finding Joy in Each Day

This is the time of year that we are thinking about setting goals. We want to be better and all of you constantly inspire me to keep trying. This brand new issue of BLOCK has been spruced up from cover to cover to start 2020 off in style! The design has been refreshed, there are exciting changes on every page, more stories from our readers, and even more enhancements to come throughout the year! We hope you love it.

Starting new also means celebrating success and recognizing growth. BLOCK has been through a lot over the past six years and so have you. I love to see how quilting changes us and helps us to become stronger. I get a lot of mail and most letters contain stories that explain how quilting has helped you get through your challenges. No matter how many trials you encounter in your lives, when you spend time at your sewing machine, you begin to put yourself back together, piece by piece. It takes time, but that journey is so sweet and then you hand off this precious quilt that you made for someone who needs some love or encouragement and you are changed.

This year I want to focus on finding joy in each day. No one thrives in negativity and so, each day, I try to look for one good thing. Instead of worrying about all the things I'm not doing, I'm going to find the things I can do. I don't think I'm going to try and finish all my UFOs or completely redo my sewing room. But I will spend more time at my sewing machine! It brings peace to my soul. You quilters continually bring hope and love into the world. Keep an eye on those around you and spread as much joy as you can!

JENNY DOAN
MISSOURI STAR QUILT CO.

Try Our App

It's easy to keep up on every issue of BLOCK magazine. Access it from all your devices. And when you subscribe to BLOCK, it's free with your subscription! For the app, search BLOCK magazine in the app store. Available for both Apple and Android.

Make Your Fabric Stash Work For *YOU*

An old saying goes, "out of sight, out of mind." Keep this in mind as you organize and make your stash as visually appealing and accessible as possible.

What's the current state of your fabric stash? Are there bins buried in the depths of your garage, attic, or basement, filled with retro fabrics? Are you unsure of what's lurking in the corners of your sewing room? Do you often discover fabrics in your stash that you have no memory of acquiring? Believe me, I'm right there with you. It's easy to buy fabric, but what you do with it when you get home makes all the difference. At the start of this brand new year, I want to make a resolution right alongside you to "shop" my stash more. At the start of a new project, instead of scrambling to find the fabrics I need, I want to walk into my sewing room with confidence and feel inspired as I look at my neatly organized stash.

The first step to fabric stash organization is the toughest part. It's time to pull out all those bins, boxes, and bolts from their hidey-holes and put them in one big heap! Seeing all your fabric in the same place will help you get a better grip on your organizational needs and remind you of how much fabric you actually have. Take a good long afternoon or a lazy Saturday and sort through your fabrics thoughtfully. Keep the ones you love and don't be afraid to donate fabrics that don't resonate any longer. They aren't serving you and they could be used by someone else.

The second step is to decide what kind of organization works for you. It all depends on how you like to use your fabrics. Do you keep collections together? Or do you sort according to color? There are many ways to do it. Personally, I keep my scrap fabrics in bins according to color, but before then, I like to organize them by collection and weight, keeping quilting cottons together and heavier fabric like canvas and minky separate.

As a quilter, I like to see what I have to work with, so organizing my stash visually is key. Use your shelves for your prettiest precuts and stack them up. Then, you might try out acrylic bolt boards or pieces of foamboard to wrap your larger pieces of fabric around. Then you can line them up on your shelf

Consider donating unwanted fabric to a good cause like your local quilt guild or a charitable organization like Quilts of Valor, Days for Girls, Project Linus, and others.

Need some guidance on how to use your fabric stash? Check out our Missouri Star Education class on stash busting. Follow this link to discover all the possibilities!

missouriquiltco.com/classes

If you frequently change sewing needles, make a needle book or use a sewing needle organizer. There's nothing worse than losing needles somewhere and "finding" them when you least expect!

like mini bolts of fabric. They look so nice! Another option is hanging up your larger pieces of fabric in an easily accessible closet on sturdy hangers.

Next up, tackle that pile of scraps! Pick out pieces of fabric you can still fold and put them into clear bins or baskets of like colors. Fabric scraps that are too small to fold can go into a bag to be used as stuffing for other projects like filling pincushions, pillows, pet beds, and so on.

Finally, notions need to be addressed. Once your fabric is sorted, take the time

to organize your notions visually as well. Arrange scissors and rotary cutters in a glass jar or a shallow tray where you can reach them (but away from small hands). Gather up loose spools of thread and display them on a thread rack or in a thread box. There's nothing worse than chasing a spool of thread across the table as it's unraveling! It's also important to store needles in a safe place, but in a way that's still easily accessible. I like to keep one pincushion for hand sewing needles and another for quilting pins and yet another for ballpoint pins. There's almost no such thing as too many pincushions. Plus, they look pretty cute on my desk.

HOW TO FOLD A FAT QUARTER

Spiff up your stash by folding neat little fat quarters. Here's how we do it at Missouri Star.

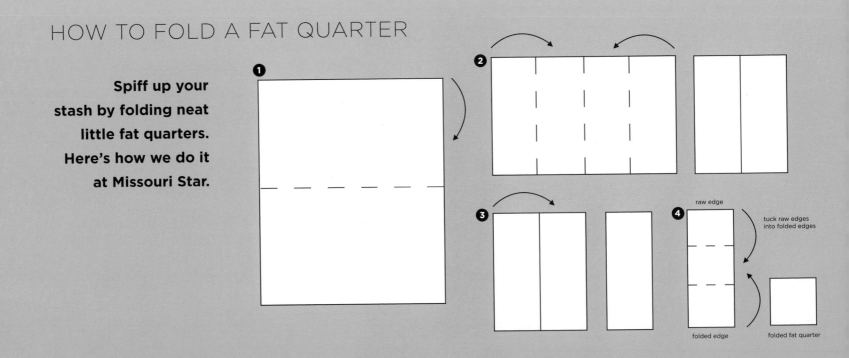

I hope these handy tips and tricks help you on your way to a bright, beautiful space for sewing. I may not always have the neatest sewing room, but I do have a wonderful helper who keeps my studio organized and I couldn't be more grateful for her. With so many projects going on at any given time, I've finally admitted that I could use a helping hand in there. Every time I step into my studio and see everything folded and put away again, it feels like magical elves have been in there, tidying and making everything sparkle and shine again. There's nothing like stepping into a freshly organized room to begin your first project of the new year and I am here to cheer you on in your efforts!

You don't need to spend a lot of money to have an organized space. Use what you have! See our instructions for turning cardboard Missouri Star shipping boxes into clever storage boxes on page 42.

What's Your Favorite Notion?
Calico Star Quilt

Fabric makes quilting fun; notions make quilting easy. From high-quality thread to innovative templates, a great set of notions makes all the difference.

We surveyed our Facebook followers to find out which notions and supplies they like best. Here are some of their answers:

"Rotary cutter and cutting mat. They are must-haves for accuracy. When I first started quilting, I traced around homemade cardboard templates, cut my pieces with scissors, and sewed everything by hand. Very labor intensive!" - *Mary W.*

Mary isn't alone in her love for rotary cutters and mats. At least half of the answers we received stated the same! Of course, we got plenty of votes for other supplies, too!

"Precuts! I adore them. My first quilt was a small baby quilt. For a beginner, cutting those itty bitty squares was a serious challenge! Precuts took away the frustration of my terrible cutting skills. I rarely buy fabric by the yard now; cutting a 10" square is far less daunting!" *-Theresa M.*

"Rotating cutting mat. I love being able to turn a block as I trim instead of lifting and misaligning the fabric." *-Rhonda R.*

"I love your 8" by 2½" template. I use it so often, I don't know how I lived without it. My latest purchase is your Missouri Star Oliso iron. I had to get my old head programmed not to stand it up, but I love how long it stays on." *-Diane B.*

"I absolutely love the Clearly Perfect Simply Slotted Trimmer for half-square triangles!" *-Suzi B.*

"My battery-operated seam ripper! So quick and easy if you have a long seam or several blocks that need to be done over. (Not that I have done that ...)" *-Yvonne M.*

"Not a notion ... my books. I have about 2 dozen books and I can look at them over and over when I want to start a new project. That and my one-year-old Bernina!" *-Barbara C.*

"I couldn't function without my quality, long glass-headed pins. Now I'm enjoying also having a thick wool pressing mat, which I just got. Nice flat seams with less effort!" *-Lin S.*

"My ¼" foot was a true game-changer. That, and Jenny's tutorials. I learned how to quilt watching her YouTube tutorials." *-Lori W.*

Several quilters mentioned Jenny's tutorials, which was such a sweet surprise! Sharing our love of quilting with the world is literally a dream come true! And with all the clever tools available, we can all become artists in our own way. Hooray for quilting that is quick, easy, and always a delight!

materials

QUILT SIZE
91" x 91"

BLOCK SIZE
24" finished

QUILT TOP
1 package 10" print squares
1 package 10" background squares
1½ yards background fabric
   - includes inner border

OUTER BORDER
1¾ yards - includes cornerstones

BINDING
¾ yard

BACKING
8¼ yards - vertical seam(s)
   or 2¾ yards of 108" wide

SAMPLE QUILT
Sun Print 2020 by Alison Glass for Andover

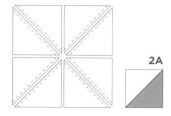

2A

1 cut

From the background fabric, cut (1) 24½" strip across the width of the fabric and set the remainder of the fabric aside for the inner border. Subcut (12) 24½" x 2½" sashing rectangles and set the remainder of the strip aside for another project.

From the outer border fabric, cut (1) 2½" strip across the width of the fabric and set the remainder of the fabric aside for the outer border. Subcut (4) 2½" squares from the strip and set the remainder aside for another project.

2 sew

Draw a line corner to corner twice on the diagonal on the reverse side of each background square. Layer a marked background square with a print square, right sides facing. Sew on both sides of each line using a ¼" seam allowance. Cut each set of sewn squares in half vertically and horizontally, then cut on the drawn lines. Open and press the seam allowance of each unit toward the darker fabric. Square each half-square triangle unit to 4½". Keep sets of 4 matching half-square triangle units together. Each set of sewn squares will yield 8 half-square triangles and a **total of 324** are needed for the quilt. **2A**

3 make broken dishes units

Select 4 matching half-square triangle units and arrange them in a 4-patch formation as shown. Sew the 2 units in the top row together and press the seam toward the right. Sew the 2 units in the bottom row together and press the seam toward the left. Nest the seams and sew the rows together to complete a broken dishes unit. **Make 36. 3A**

4 make chevron units

Select 4 matching half-square triangle

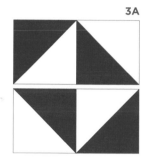

3A

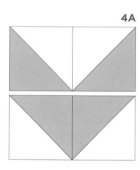

4A

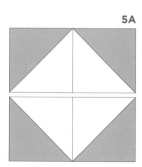

5A

units and arrange them in a 4-patch formation as shown. Sew the 2 units in the top row together and press the seam toward the right. Sew the 2 units in the bottom row together and press the seam toward the left. Nest the seams and sew the rows together to complete a chevron unit. **Make 36. 4A**

5 make diamond units

Select 4 matching half-square triangle units and arrange them in a 4-patch formation as shown. Sew the 2 units in the top row together and press the seam toward the right. Sew the 2 units in the bottom row together and press the seam toward the left. Nest the seams and sew the rows together to complete a diamond unit. **Make 9. 5A**

Note: You will have 12 half-square triangles that can be set aside for another project after you have sewn the broken dishes, chevron, and diamond units.

6 make the blocks

Pick up 4 broken dishes units, 4 chevron units, and 1 diamond unit. Arrange the units into a 9-patch formation as shown. Sew the units together in rows. **6A**

Press the seams of the top and bottom rows to the right. Press the seams of the middle row to the left. Nest the seams and sew the rows together to complete the block. **Make 9. 6B**

Block Size: 24" finished

7 make horizontal sashing strips

Pick up the sashing rectangles and 2½" squares cut from the outer border fabric. Sew a square to both ends of a sashing rectangle. Sew a sashing rectangle to each end of the unit. Press all of the seams towards the rectangles

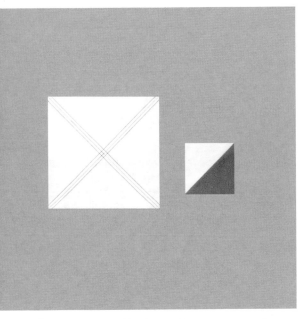

1 Lay a marked background square atop a print square, right sides facing. Sew on both sides of each line. Cut the sewn square in half vertically and horizontally, then along both drawn lines. Open and press each unit towards the darker fabric. Repeat to make 324 half-square triangles.

2 Select 4 matching half-square triangles and arrange them as shown. Sew the units together in pairs to form rows. Nest the seams and sew the rows together. Press to complete a broken dishes unit. Make 4.

3 Select 4 matching half-square triangles and arrange them as shown. Sew the units together in pairs to form rows. Nest the seams and sew the rows together. Press to complete a chevron unit. Make 4.

4 Select 4 matching half-square triangles and arrange them as shown. Sew the units together in pairs to form rows. Nest the seams and sew the rows together. Press to complete the diamond unit.

5 Arrange the 4 broken dishes units, 4 chevron units, and 1 diamond unit into 3 rows of 3 units as shown. Sew the units together to form rows.

6 Nest the seams and sew the 3 rows together. Press to complete the block.

6A

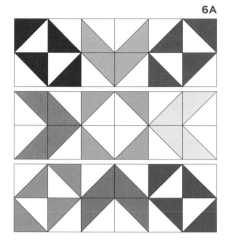

6B

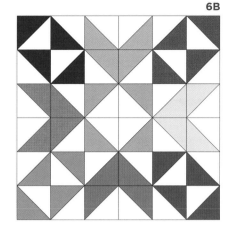

7A

to complete the horizontal sashing strip. **Make 2. 7A**

8 arrange & sew

Lay out the blocks in **3 rows** with each row being made up of **3 blocks**. As you make each row, sew a sashing rectangle between each block. Press the seam allowances toward the sashing rectangles. Refer to the diagram to the left if necessary.

Sew the rows together adding a horizontal sashing strip between each row.

9 inner border

Cut (8) 2½" strips across the width of the background fabric. Sew the strips together end-to-end to make 1 long strip. Trim the inner borders from this strip.

Refer to Borders (pg. 102) in the Construction Basics to measure and cut the inner borders. The strips are approximately 76½" for the sides and 80½" for the top and bottom.

10 outer border

Cut (9) 6" strips across the width of the fabric. Sew the strips together end-to-end to make 1 long strip. Trim the outer borders from this strip.

Refer to Borders (pg. 102) in the Construction Basics to measure and cut the outer borders. The strips are approximately 80½" for the sides and 91½" for the top and bottom.

11 quilt & bind

Layer the quilt with batting and backing and quilt. After the quilting is complete, square up the quilt and trim away all excess batting and backing. Add binding to complete the quilt. See Construction Basics (pg. 102) for binding instructions.

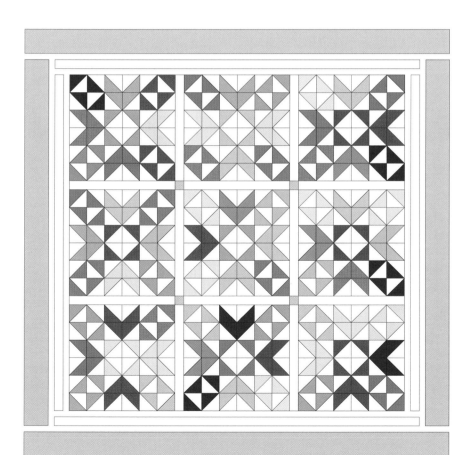

Resizing the Calico Star Block
Calico Star Mini Block + Pillow

Aren't tiny things precious? I can't help but squeal when I see miniature versions of sewing notions or adorable doll quilts. Many of you may know that I am a collector and I have gathered up quite a few little toy sewing machines. They just make me smile. Well, for this fun tutorial reboot, we've taken one of my favorite quilt blocks from this issue and shrunk it down to a new, cute size! The Calico Star block was originally a big, beautiful half-square triangle quilt block measuring two feet wide, but in this version, it's a petite 9" block.

Sizing down a quilt pattern isn't as hard as you might imagine, especially when you're using precuts. They take out the guesswork! Because the original Calico Star block was made with 10" squares, in the small version, we used 5" squares. You follow all the same directions, so don't fret much if your block turns out a little bigger or a little smaller than you expected. Remember what I always say about seam allowances. It's better to be consistent than perfect, so if you tend to use a scant ¼" seam allowance, your block may turn out a bit bigger and that's totally okay.

Here are some new color options for this fun-sized block. It's incredible how different fabrics change the way a quilt block looks. Consider the number of colors you include, the size of your prints, your background color, color placement, and fabric contrast. All of these elements can add variety to an already familiar quilt block. Also, think about how you finish up your quilt. Different quilting styles can emphasize certain aspects of your design and give your project a brand new feel from traditional meandering quilting motifs to straight-line modern quilting designs. How do you like to finish your quilt?

Then, when you're all done creating your very own Calico Star quilt, keep on stitching and make a cute pillow to match! This mini version of the original quilt block is perfect for a home decor project. After you make your quilt, you can take any leftovers or test blocks, add a border, create a quick pillow, and toss it on the sofa to brighten up your living room. This darling pillow is so easy to make, you might end up with more throw pillows than you have room on your couch!

Get creative choosing your fabrics and this quilt block will become yours and reflect your personal style. Share your version of the Calico Star mini quilt with us at #msqcshowandtell.

SOLID BLOCK

Solids make this block feel fresh and modern in bright, happy colors. The great thing about solids is they all match! There's no need to fuss about print direction or size—they make quilting friendly and fun.

2-COLOR BLOCK

Sunny batik fabrics are used to create a two-color palette in yellow and white. Two colors are always classic and simple. It gives the focus to the pattern and allows for greater contrast. Now, what would happen if you switched the background fabric with the main fabric?

3-COLOR BLOCK

These three batik fabrics go from light in the center to dark at the edges for a dynamic look. Choosing three colors in light, medium, and dark hue allows for a gradation in contrast. What might this block look like if it went from dark to light instead?

SCRAPPY BLOCK

Use a variety of primitive style fabrics for a homespun, scrappy effect. This is a great project for scrap busting. All you need is an assorted bunch of 5″ squares and your choice of background square color. In this case, we went with a neutral cream.

Calico Star Mini Pillow

materials

PROJECT SIZE: fits a 16" pillow form
BLOCK SIZE: 9" finished

PROJECT SUPPLIES
(9) 5" dark print squares
(9) 5" light print squares
1 yard coordinating print - includes
   borders and pillow back
18" square of batting

OPTIONAL PILLOW INSERT
½ yard muslin
Fiberfill

Don't have a pillow form handy? Simply cut (2) 17" squares of fabric and sew them together around the perimeter using a ½" seam allowance with right sides facing. Leave an opening about 4-6" wide for turning. Clip the corners and turn right side out. Stuff the pillow with fiberfill and whipstitch the opening closed.

1 sew the block

Follow the directions on page 14 to make a Calico Star block. Simply replace the 10" squares with the 5" squares listed here. Each set of 5" squares will yield 8 half-square triangle units. Set 4 half-square triangles aside for another project. Square the remaining units to 2" and keep them in sets of 4 matching units.

Keep following the Calico Star directions to make 4 broken dishes units, 4 chevron units, and 1 diamond unit. Now use those 9 units to put a mini Calico Star block together. **1A**

Block Size: 9" finished

2 cut

From the coordinating fabric, cut (1) 20" strip across the width of the fabric. Subcut (1) 20" square. From the remainder of the strip, cut (4) 4" strips. From the 4" strips, subcut (2) 4" x 9½" rectangles and (2) 4" x 16½" rectangles.

From the coordinating fabric, cut an 11½" strip across the width of the fabric. Subcut (2) 11½" x 17" rectangles.

3 finish the pillow top

Sew a 4" x 9½" rectangle to 2 opposite sides of the block and press the seam allowances towards the rectangles. Sew a 4" x 16½" rectangle to the remaining sides of the block and press the seam allowances towards the rectangles to finish the pillow top. **3A**

Layer your pillow top on top of the batting and backing square. Baste and quilt using your favorite methods. After the quilting is complete, square up and trim away all excess batting and backing.

4 make the pillow back

Fold a long edge of an 11½" x 17" rectangle over ½" with wrong sides touching. Press. Repeat a second time to enclose the raw edge of the fabric. Topstitch along the folded edge. Repeat on 1 long edge of the remaining rectangle to create the 2 pillow back flaps. **4A**

5 finish the pillow

Lay the pillow top with the right side facing up. Lay the 2 pillow back flaps on top of the pillow top. **5A**

Note: The right sides of the pillow back flaps should be touching the right side of the pillow top and the pillow back flaps should overlap each other by about 4".

Pin or clip the pillow back flaps to the pillow top. Sew around the perimeter of the pillow using a ½" seam allowance. Finish the edges with a serger or zigzag stitch to prevent fraying.

Clip the corners and turn the pillow right sides out. Insert a pillow form to finish your project.

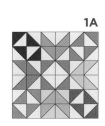

1A

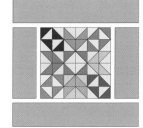

3A

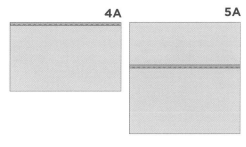

4A   5A

Sharing the Quilting Love
Happy Hearts Quilt

It's a cozy February here in Hamilton and I'm definitely feeling the love. There are so many reasons my heart is full and your endless support is always one of them. I've got a well-worn quilt wrapped around me, an English paper piecing project on my lap, and my husband is puttering away on some project in the garage. All is right in the world, for now. But I know that isn't always the case in our lives. Whether we are in the midst of turmoil, or we are in a peaceful place, there is always a way to strengthen ourselves and keep going. I think it's possible to have a happy heart even when life is tough, and a couple of ways I try to maintain my sense of optimism is expressing my creativity and living generously. I know we don't always have a lot to give of our possessions, but we do have so much we can give from the heart.

Sharing our love of quilting reaches further than we might ever imagine. Have you ever picked up a vintage quilt in a thrift store and wondered who stitched it together all those years ago? It continues on, providing warmth and comfort, even though the maker may be long gone. Quilting isn't about having the biggest fabric stash or the best tools, it's about creating something handmade, and the time we take to make things ourselves really does count for something. It expresses our generosity and love through time and patience. There is so little of this in the world today. Take time to savor each stitch and share your talents with others.

Passing on your skills to others is also a way to show you care. I've heard many stories about how quilting is passed down through the generations. One reader, Lora Conners, sent in her story.

"One of my greatest blessings was my grandmother. She started me on my sewing journey when I was a young girl. Some of my memories of her include seeing her beautiful quilts. She would get them out of her dressers and she would tell me their stories. The beautiful colors and patterns were so lovely and each one was created with so much love. I was absolutely hooked!

"I started out making clothes for my dolls and graduated to clothes for my children. During the years I was a busy mother of four, my intentions of making my own quilts had to take a back seat, but the desire was always there!

"I am so pleased to tell you I have fulfilled that dream and have an even greater appreciation of my grandmother's quilts and wonderful stories! I name my quilts and they are creations from my heart and soul. I was recently bestowed the honor of setting together and finishing a grandmother's flower garden quilt. The pieces were over 100 years old and still beautifully intact.

"I am forever grateful that my grandmother took the time to show me her beautiful quilts and instill in me how very special they truly are, as well as the people who make them!"

Quilters, you may never know what you do by sharing your passion for quilting with others. Your quilts might spark someone's creativity tomorrow or it might bless someone generations ahead of you. Making beautiful things and taking the time to show you care creates a ripple effect. All that love ripples out from a single act, creating waves that continue on and on.

materials

QUILT SIZE
73" x 73"

BLOCK SIZE
30" finished

QUILT TOP
1 package 10" print squares
1 package 10" background squares

INNER BORDER
¾ yard

OUTER BORDER
1¼ yards

BINDING
¾ yard

BACKING
4½ yards - vertical seam(s)
    or 2¼ yards of 108" wide

SAMPLE QUILT
Petals and Pots by Gabrielle Niel Design
Studio for Riley Blake Designs

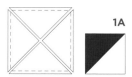

1A

1 sew

Select (25) 10″ print squares and (25) 10″ background squares and set the rest of the squares aside for another project.

Layer a background square on top of a print square with right sides facing. Sew around the 4 sides of the stacked squares using a ¼″ seam allowance. Cut the sewn squares on each diagonal and open to reveal 4 half-square triangle units. Press the seams of each unit toward the darker fabric and trim as needed. Repeat to **make 100** half-square triangle units. **1A**

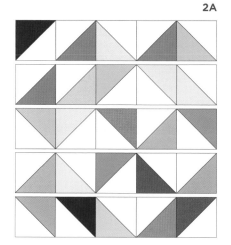

2A

2 block construction

Select 25 half-square triangles and arrange them into **5 rows** of **5 units** as shown. Sew the units together in rows. Press the seams of the odd-numbered rows to the right and the seams of the even-numbered rows to the left. **2A**

Nest the seams and sew the rows together to complete the block. **Make 4. 2B**

Block Size: 30″ finished

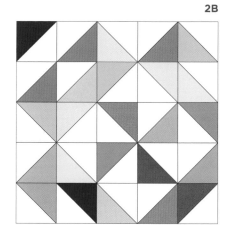

2B

3 arrange & sew

Lay out the blocks in **2 rows** with each row being made of **2 blocks**, making note of the orientation of the blocks in the diagram on page 27 as needed. Sew the blocks together to form rows. Press the seam allowance of the top row to the right and the seam allowance of the bottom row to the left.

Nest the seams and sew the rows together.

4 inner border

Cut (7) 2½″ strips across the width of the background fabric. Sew the strips together end-to-end to make 1 long strip. Trim the inner borders from this strip.

Refer to Borders (pg. 102) in the Construction Basics to measure and cut the inner borders. The strips are approximately 60½″ for the sides and 64½″ for the top and bottom.

5 outer border

Cut (7) 5″ strips across the width of the fabric. Sew the strips together end-to-end to make 1 long strip. Trim the outer borders from this strip.

Refer to Borders (pg. 102) in the Construction Basics to measure and cut the outer borders. The strips are approximately 64½″ for the sides and 73½″ for the top and bottom.

6 quilt & bind

Layer the quilt with batting and backing and quilt. After the quilting is complete, square up the quilt and trim away all excess batting and backing. Add binding to complete the quilt. See Construction Basics (pg. 102) for binding instructions.

1 Lay a background square atop a print square with right sides facing. Sew around all 4 sides of the stacked squares with a ¼" seam allowance.

2 Cut the sewn square on both diagonals. Each sewn square will yield 4 half-square triangles.

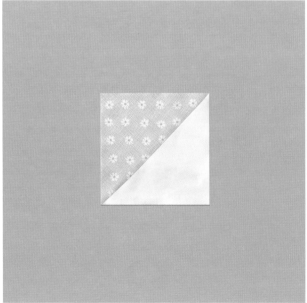

3 Press the seam of each half-square triangle towards the darker fabric. Repeat until you have made 100 half-square triangles.

4 Layout 25 half-square triangle units in 5 rows of 5 units as shown to form a quadrant of the quilt. Make 4 quadrants.

Quilting: A Real Pain in the Neck?

Around the Square Quilt

Quilting for hours is a delight. That is, until you try to stand up. Suddenly, you discover there's a crick in your neck, your back is throbbing, your arms are stiff, and your legs have nearly forgotten how to walk! But friends, it doesn't have to be that way! With just a few adjustments to your habits and your sewing room, you can sew to your heart's delight and feel good, too!

Choose the right chair: Sit all the way back. (You may have the tendency to scoot up to the edge of the seat. Don't do it!) Make sure your chair has great lumbar support, and adjust the height so your knees are just a little lower than your hips. Every body is different. Be sure to test the fit before buying a new chair.

Don't slouch

Your sewing machine, ironing board, and cutting table should all fit YOU. A good rule of thumb is to have these surfaces adjusted to elbow-height so you don't have to bend over to work.

Light it up

Fill your sewing room with plenty of lighting to avoid eye strain. There are easy and affordable LED lights you can attach to your machine if the light is insufficient. And don't hesitate to use a magnifying glass for those pesky little seams.

Take frequent breaks

A chiropractor friend of mine advised, "Before you sit down to quilt, drink a full bottle of water. Before long, you'll have to take a bathroom break. When you use the creative side of your brain, time flies. You have to set a timer … or drink that water … to force yourself to get up and move. Make a snack, do a few stretches, take a stroll to the mailbox. Then drink another bottle of water and start quilting again."

Like most quilters, I spend a lot of time sitting in a chair. But I know our bodies work so much better when we are moving. Like you, I want to keep sewing for many years, so this year I'm making it a point to get up and move more often.

I am always so inspired by the quilters who come to Hamilton for a retreat. Each morning before they start sewing, several will get together and take a walk. It's just 15 to 30 minutes, but such a wonderful way to start the day and take care of their bodies.

Quilters are some of the most selfless people I know. Always doing and giving; always taking care of other people. But remember, it's important to take care of yourself as well. You need it, and you deserve it, too!

materials

QUILT SIZE
78" x 78"

BLOCK SIZE
7" finished

QUILT TOP
1 package 10" print squares*
1 package 10" background squares

INNER BORDER
¾ yards - matching background squares

OUTER BORDER
1½ yards

BINDING
¾ yard

BACKING
4¾ yards - vertical seam(s)** or 2½ yards 108" wide

OTHER
Missouri Star Quilt Company Small Simple Wedge Template

*Note: You will need (41) 10" print squares that contrast your background fabric. If your package has some squares that do not contrast, you'll need to replace those squares with 10" squares cut from a coordinating print fabric. Different coordinating fabric can be used and up to (4) 10" squares can be cut from each ½ yard.

**Note: Backing fabric must have 42" of usable width.

SAMPLE QUILT
Cherry Lemonade by Jason Yenter for In the Beginning Fabrics

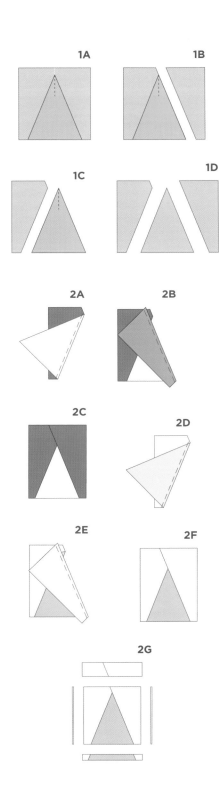

1 cut

Select 41 each of your print squares and background squares. Set the remaining print and background squares aside for another project.

Cut each of the selected squares in half vertically and horizontally to create (4) 5" squares from each. Keep the print squares in matching sets of 4.

Select (1) 5" square, fold it in half lengthwise, and finger-press the 1 edge of the fold. Open the square and lay it right side up on your cutting surface with the crease at the top. Lay the template on top of the square, lining up the bottom edges, and lining up the dashed line at the top of the template with your creased center mark. **1A**

Carefully trim all the way along the right side of the template creating a right side triangle. Left-handed? See note about * below. **1B**

Move the right side triangle you just cut out of the way. Without disturbing the template and fabric, trim along the left side of the template creating a left side triangle and a wedge. **1C**

Repeat the previous cutting instructions for the remaining 5" print and background squares to create both print and background sets of right side triangles, left side triangles, and wedges. Be sure to cut the right side first each time. See * below. **1D**

***Note:** Left-handed cutters may prefer to cut the left side first each time. If you cut the left side first, the right side triangle will need to be sewn first when making wedge units.

2 make wedge units

Unit A

You will need 1 background wedge, 1 left side print triangle, and 1 right side print triangle to make each Unit A. Take a left side print triangle and lay it right side up.

Lay a background wedge, wrong side up, on top of the left side triangle as shown. Sew along the right edge using a ¼" seam allowance. **2A**

Open and press the seam allowance toward the darker fabric. Lay the right side print triangle on top of the pieced unit, right sides together, and lining up the right edges as shown. Sew along the right edge using a ¼" seam allowance. **2B**

Open and press the seam allowance toward the darker fabric. Repeat sewing background wedges and print triangle sets to make a **total of 164** of Unit A. **2C**

Keep units in sets of 4 matching units.

Unit B

You will need 1 print wedge, 1 left side background triangle, and 1 right side background triangle to make each Unit B. Take a left side background triangle and lay it right side up. Lay a print wedge, wrong side up, on top of the left side triangle as shown. Sew along the right edge using a ¼" seam allowance. **2D**

Open and press the seam allowance toward the darker fabric. Lay the right side background triangle on top of the pieced unit, right sides together, and lining up the right edges as shown. Sew along the right edge using a ¼" seam allowance. **2E**

Open and press the seam allowance toward the darker fabric. Repeat sewing background wedges and print triangle sets to make a **total of 160** of Unit B. **2F**

Keep units in sets of 4 matching units.

Trim each Unit A and Unit B to 4" square by trimming the top first, leaving ½" above the point of the wedge. Trim the bottom as needed. Measure 2" from both sides of the wedge point and trim either side as needed. **2G**

3A

3B

3C

3D

3 block construction

Arrange 4 of Unit A into a 4-patch formation as shown. Sew the units together in rows. **3A**

Press the seams of the top row to the left and the bottom row to the right. Nest the seams and sew the rows together to complete the block. **Make 41** of Block A. **3B**

Block Size: 7″ finished

Arrange 4 of Unit B into a 4-patch formation as shown. Sew the units together in rows. **3C**

Press the seams of the top row to the left and the bottom row to the right. Nest the seams and sew the rows together to complete the block. **Make 40** of Block B. **3D**

Block Size: 7″ finished

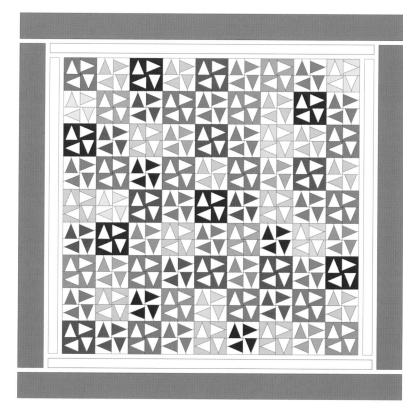

4 arrange & sew

Referring to the diagram below, lay out your blocks in **9 rows** of **9 blocks** each. Each row will alternate Block A and Block B. Sew the blocks together in rows. Press the seam allowances of all the odd-numbered rows to the left and all the even-numbered rows to the right. Nest the seams and sew the rows together.

5 inner border

Cut (7) 2½″ strips across the width of the fabric. Sew the strips end-to-end to make 1 long strip.

Refer to Borders (pg. 102) in the Construction Basics to measure and cut the inner borders. The strips are approximately 63½″ for the sides and approximately 67½″ for the top and bottom.

6 outer border

Cut (8) 6″ strips across the width of the fabric. Sew the strips together end-to-end to make 1 long strip. Trim the borders from this strip.

Refer to Borders (pg. 102) in the Construction Basics to measure and cut the outer borders. The strips are approximately 67½″ for the sides and approximately 78½″ for the top and bottom.

7 quilt & bind

Layer the quilt with batting and backing and quilt. After the quilting is complete, square up the quilt and trim away all excess batting and backing. Add binding to complete the quilt. See Construction Basics (pg. 102) for binding instructions.

Change Can Be Good
Cottage Stars Table Runner

At the heart of things, people are creatures of comfort. We enjoy knowing what's going to happen, so we can keep using our plans and habits and not have to think too hard about it. Oftentimes, we think we'd be fine if things stayed just as they are. "Things are comfortable now," you say. You know that if things were to change, you'd have to make new plans and put a bunch of effort into it, and who wants to do that? But, no matter what we want life to be like, life is a series of changes. Friends come and go, family grows and shrinks, and new situations face us at every turn. Even though change is inevitable, we're always most comfortable when things stay as they are.

But, change can be good! Every new situation is an opportunity to grow, and, if you work at it, you can make those changes for the better. And sometimes, you need to make those changes happen yourself. What was once comfortable starts to become stale, and we get stuck in "the daily grind." Eventually, knowing exactly how your day, week, or month is going to go just drains you, because, as much as we are creatures of habit, we are also curious and adventure-seeking! Sometimes you just have to get a change of scenery, take up a new project, or pack up and move across the country to shake up the routine. When we roll with the changes, we can find new and wonderful things about the world and ourselves.

We asked around about how others make the best of change. Lavonne Lessard wrote to us, saying:

"I taught quilting to military young wives in Vicenza, Italy. I remember quilting with my aunt when I was a young girl. I needed a job, and I was asked if I could teach quilting when a quilting teacher job opened up. I had not quilted since I was 16 years old. Now, I'm in my 50s and found myself craving to renew the art within myself.

"I quickly took to YouTube looking desperately for any help I could find to assist me in teaching these women how to sew and how to quilt and yet be enthusiastic about the whole process. Thank God for Missouri Star Quilt and Jenny! I took to those videos like a cat to a tuna can. I was enchanted at how easy quilting had become!

"I passed this new knowledge onto my students, my class curriculum, and like magic, these young girls became curious about this new craft and I had a faithful following of ladies! Quilting became part of our life in Vicenza! It helped us endure the five-year term there. It saved my soul and formed new friendships with those young women."

See? Change can, well, change things and make them turn out for the best. So, go make some changes in your life and shake things up! You might be surprised at how well it turns out.

materials

PROJECT SIZE
36" x 17"

BLOCK SIZES
4" x 5½" finished and 6" finished

PROJECT TOP
1 package 5" print squares
½ yard background fabric

BINDING
¼ yard

BACKING
¾ yard

SAMPLE QUILT
Painterly Petals by Studio RK for Robert Kaufman Fabrics

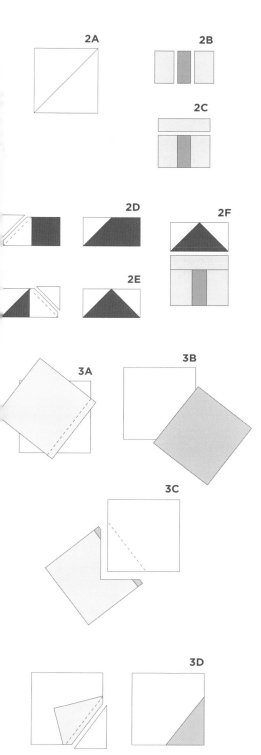

2A 2B 2C 2D 2F 2E 3A 3B 3C 3D

1 sort & cut

Select (18) 5" print squares to use for the houses. Cut a 1½" strip across the width of a square. Subcut (1) 1½" x 4½" rectangle for the top of a house. Trim the remainder of the fabric left from the square to measure 3" x 5", then subcut into (2) 2" x 3" rectangles. Keep the 3 rectangles together. Repeat to cut the additional 17 selected 5" print squares.

Select (6) 5" print squares to use for the doors of the houses. Cut a 3" strip across the width of each 5" square. Subcut the strip into (3) 1½" x 3" rectangles. A **total of 18** door rectangles are needed.

Select (9) 5" print squares to use for the roofs of the houses. Cut each square in half to yield 2 rectangles. Trim each rectangle to measure 2½" x 4½".

Select (8) 5" print squares to use for the wonky stars and set the remaining square aside for another project. Cut each 5" square in half vertically and horizontally to yield (4) 2½" squares. A **total of (30)** 2½" squares are needed for the wonky stars.

From the background fabric, cut:

- Cut (6) 2½" strips across the width of the fabric. Subcut each strip into 2½" squares. Each full strip will yield 16 squares and a **total of 84** are needed.

2 make tiny houses

Mark a diagonal line on the reverse side of (36) 2½" background squares. **2A**

Select a set of 3 matching rectangles, 1 door rectangle, 1 roof rectangle, and 2 background squares. Be sure the rectangles you select are cut from different fabrics for the house, the door, and the roof. Sew the (2) 2" x 3" rectangles to either side of the 1½" x 3" door rectangle. Press the seam allowances away from the door rectangle. **2B**

Sew the 1½" x 4½" rectangle to the top of the unit. Press the seam towards the top and set this house unit aside for a moment. **2C**

Lay a marked background square on the left side of the roof rectangle with right sides facing as shown. Sew on the marked line. Trim away the excess fabric ¼" from the sewn seam. Open and press towards the corner. **2D**

Lay the other marked background square on the right side of the roof rectangle with right sides facing as shown. Sew on the marked line and trim away the excess fabric ¼" from the sewn seam. Open and press towards the corner to complete the roof unit. **2E**

Pick up the house unit you set aside earlier. Sew it to the bottom of the roof unit you just made. Press the seam towards the bottom to complete the block. **Make 18** blocks. **2F**

Block Size: 4" x 5½" finished

3 make wonky stars

Select (6) 2½" print squares to use in the center of the stars and (24) 2½" background squares and set them aside for the moment. Use the remaining 2½" print squares and 2½" background squares to make the star legs.

Place a 2½" print square on an angle (any angle) atop a 2½" background square with right sides facing. Make sure your print square is placed a little past the halfway point. Sew ¼" in from the angled edge of the print square. **3A**

1 Sew a door rectangle between a pair of matching 2″ x 3″ rectangles. Press the seams outwards. Sew the matching 1½″ x 4½″ rectangle to the top of the unit and press the seam upwards to create a house unit.

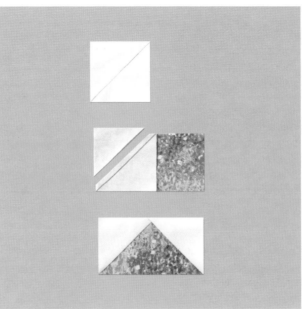

2 Mark a diagonal line on the reverse side of a background square. Place the square on the left corner of a roof rectangle and sew along the marked line. Trim away the excess fabric and press towards the corner. Repeat to snowball the other side of the rectangle to make a roof unit.

3 Sew the roof unit to the top of the house unit. Press the seam towards the bottom to complete the block.

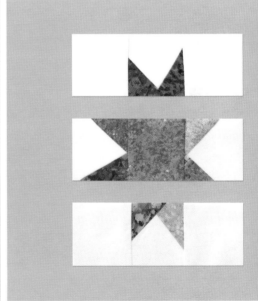

4 Place a 2½″ print square on top of a 2½″ background square at an angle with right sides facing. At any angle with right sides facing. The print square should cross over the center of the bottom edge of the background square. Fold the print square over the seam and press.

5 Turn the piece over and use the background square as a guide to trim the excess print fabric away. Fold the print fabric back and trim ¼″ away from the seam. Add another star leg just like before using another print square.

6 Arrange 4 star leg squares, 4 background squares, and 1 print square in 3 rows of 3 units as shown and sew together in rows. Press the seams of the top and bottom row towards the background squares. Press the seams of the middle row towards the print square.

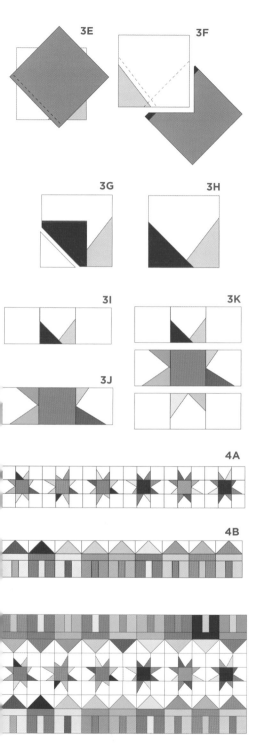

Press the piece flat to set the seam, then press the print piece over the seam allowance. **3B**

Turn the unit over and use the background square as a guide to trim the print fabric so that all of the edges are even. Save the trimmed scrap to use for another leg of the star. (You should be able to make at least 2 star legs from each print square.) **3C**

Turn the unit back over so that the right side of the fabric is facing up. Fold the print fabric of the star leg back to reveal the seam allowance and trim the excess background fabric ¼" away from the sewn seam. Fold the star leg back so the right side of the fabric is facing up and press. **3D**

Place another print square or a trimmed print scrap on the adjacent side of the square. Make sure the edge of the second print piece crosses over the first star leg by at least ¼". Stitch ¼" in from the edge of the print piece. **3E**

Press the print piece over the seam allowance. Turn the unit over and use the background square as a guide to trim the print fabric so all of the edges are even. Notice your square is still 2½". **3F**

Turn the unit back over so that the right side of the fabric is facing up. Fold the print fabric of the star leg back to reveal the seam allowance and trim the excess fabric ¼" away from the sewn seam. **3G**

Fold the star leg back so the right side of the fabric is facing up and press. **Make 24** star leg squares. **Note:** Have fun with this and don't try to make all of the star legs alike! **3H**

Sew a background square to either side of a star leg square. Press the seams towards the background squares. **Make 12. 3I**

Sew a star leg square to either side of each print square you set aside earlier. Make sure the star legs point away from the center square. Press the seams toward the center square. **3J**

Nest the seams and sew the rows together to complete the block. **Make 6** blocks. **3K**

Block Size: 6" finished

4 arrange & sew
Arrange the 6 wonky star blocks into a row. Sew the blocks together and press the seams to 1 side. **4A**

Select 9 tiny house blocks and arrange them into a single row. Sew the blocks together and press the seams towards the right. Make a second row, but press the seams of this row towards the left. **4B**

Arrange the 3 rows together as shown in the diagram on the bottom left. Be sure to make note of the orientation of the tiny house blocks. Nest the seams and sew the rows together. Press to complete the table runner top.

5 quilt & bind
Layer the table runner top with batting and backing and quilt. After the quilting is complete, square up the project and trim away all excess batting and backing. Add binding to complete the table runner. See Construction Basics (pg. 102) for binding instructions.

Create Stylish Storage Boxes for Your Fabric

Instead of spending a little too much on a fancy storage basket, why not repurpose that shipping box into a custom fabric-covered storage box that will complement your sewing room.

Have you recently ordered some fabric from Missouri Star? Before you recycle your cardboard box, hang onto it because we have a fun way to use it that will actually help keep your stash in check! Instead of spending a little too much on a fancy storage basket, why not repurpose that shipping box into a custom fabric-covered storage box that will complement your sewing room. You can cover it with practically any fabric you like and after a few more shipments of fabric, you'll have an entire set to organize your fabric, notions, books, patterns, and anything else you can think of!

Fabric-Covered Storage Boxes

materials

Fabric of your choice

1 box* of your choice
Cutting mat
Rotary cutter
Ruler

*Note: This pattern will only work for boxes that measure less than 40" around the perimeter of the box.

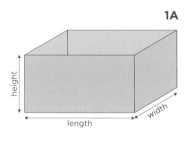

1A

3A

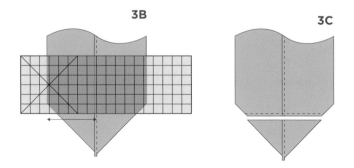

3B

3C

1 measure

Select the box you'd like to cover and let's figure out how much fabric you'll need to cover it. **1A**

Start by measuring the height of your box and multiplying your number by 2. Write your answer down.

Next, measure the shortest side or width of the box and divide this number by 2. Write your answer down.

Add your 2 answers together. Add 1 more inch and you have just calculated the size of the fabric strip you will need to cover and line your box.

2 cut

Fold your fabric in half lengthwise (selvage to selvage) and lay it flat on your cutting surface. Cut a strip across the width of the fabric to the height you determined above.

Flatten your box in half and line up the side edge of the box along the fold of the fabric. Trim the fabric strip ¼" away from the side of the box on the end opposite the fold.

3 sew

Refold your fabric with the right sides together. Sew along the side and bottom edges of your fabric using a ¼" seam allowance. **3A**

With the sewn fabric still right sides together, use both hands to pinch and pull apart the corner. As you pull, the fabric will begin to form a little peak with the corner point at the top and the seam running down the middle. Align the side and bottom seams. Place a pin in the matched seams to hold them together as it is important these stay matched up so you have nice and square corners.

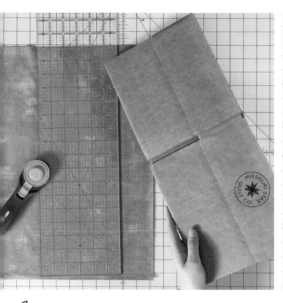

1 Gather your supplies.

2 Measure the height of your box. Do not include any flaps that will be folded inside the box in your measurement.

3 Line up the seams to form a peak in the corner. Measure half of the width of your box down from the point and make a mark. Draw a line perpendicular to the seams across the corner at this point.

Look back at the numbers you wrote down earlier. You'll need to know the second answer you wrote down (box width ÷ 2) for boxing the corners of your fabric. Find your measurement on your ruler and place that point on the center seam of your fabric. Gently slide the ruler up along the seam of your fabric until the end of the ruler reaches the angled fold of the fabric. Stop moving once you reach that point and ensure that the ruler is 90° to the seam line. Once you've determined you're in the right place, mark a line along your ruler on both sides of the seam. Repeat for the remaining side. **3B**

Note: The second side will not have a seam to match as this is where the fold was. Match the fold in the fabric to the seam on the bottom.

Sew along the marked lines and trim the excess fabric ¼″ away from the sewn seams. **3C**

Fold the raw edge along the perimeter of the fabric over ½″ to the wrong side and press. Repeat to enclose the raw edges within the fold of the fabric. Topstitch in place. **3D**

With the right side of the fabric on the inside, place the lining inside the box. Push the corners of the lining into the corners of the box. Fold the fabric down over the outside of the box. **3E 3F**

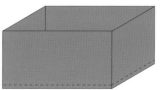

3D

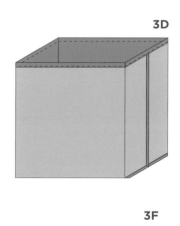

3E

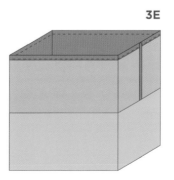

3F

43

A Quilt for Adventures
Summer Stars Quilt

Balmy summer nights are perfect for weddings. Surrounded by fresh flowers, twinkling lights, soft music, and good friends, it's so wonderful to bask in the glow of young love. I adore seeing these sweet couples just starting out on their life's journey together and because I am blessed with many children and grandchildren, I have had the privilege of being invited to many lovely weddings over the years.

My grandson Isaac and his wife Aislinn were recently married and it was an event to remember! I wanted to give them a gift they would cherish and, of course, I made them a quilt. Now, I've seen all kinds of quilts at weddings: Perfectly color-coordinated to the theme, large ornate heirloom quilts, cozy flannel quilts, and I even knew a couple who used a quilt as their guestbook. What a clever idea! They had guests sign each square and when they were through, it was all made into a quilt for them to treasure.

No matter what kind of quilt you like to give, I'm sure it will be loved. Personally, I want my quilt to be used—thrown on the living room floor for a casual movie night or draped over the kitchen table by the kids to make a blanket fort. I try to give anyone in my family who's getting married a picnic quilt in a cute picnic basket and admonish them to keep dating for the rest of their lives.

The nice thing about a picnic quilt is that by calling it by that name, they now have permission to use it for more than a decoration. It can be used for an impromptu picnic out on the front lawn, for cuddling a sniffling, sick child, for playing a game of peek-a-boo, and for any of life's adventures they can dream up!

My hope is that this quilt won't be kept carefully wrapped up in a locked cedar chest. I want them to keep it in their car and take it wherever they go. I want them to pull it out during long road trips and take it to the beach. I like knowing that my quilt will not live on a shelf in a closet or at the bottom of a hope chest, but it will be well-used and well-loved.

The quilt I made for Isaac and Aislinn was created in a blue and white color palette, using the same pattern as this Summer Stars quilt. What upcoming events are you planning for this year? Whether you've got a new baby coming into the family, a graduate leaving for college, a couple getting married, or a special birthday on the way, a quilt is always a beautiful, useful gift.

materials

QUILT SIZE
60" x 72"

BLOCK SIZES
11" finished and 6" finished

QUILT TOP
1 roll 2½" print strips
1 yard background fabric
 - includes inner border

OUTER BORDER
1½ yards

BINDING
¾ yard

BACKING
3¾ yards - horizontal seam(s)

OTHER
Clearly Perfect Slotted Trimmer - B

SAMPLE QUILT
Flour Garden by Linzee Kull McCray for
Moda Fabrics

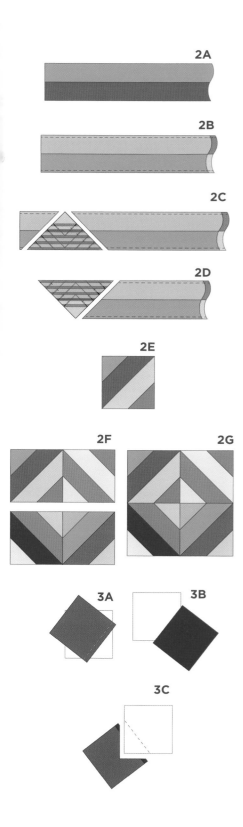

2A

2B

2C

2D

2E

2F 2G

3A 3B

3C

1 sort & cut

Select (32) 2½" print strips for the Summer in the Park blocks. Set these aside for the moment. Select (5) 2½" print strips for wonky star blocks. Set the remaining strips aside for another project.

Cut 4 wonky star print strips into (16) 2½" squares. Cut (6) 2½" squares from the remaining wonky star print strip and set the rest of the strip aside for another project. You will need a **total of (70)** 2½" squares. Set the 2½" squares aside for the moment.

From the background fabric, cut (1) 1½" strip across the width of the fabric. Subcut a **total of (4)** 1½" x 6½" background rectangles. Set the rectangles aside for the wonky star rows.

From the background fabric cut (13) 2½" strips across the width of the fabric. Set 6 background strips aside for the inner border. From the 7 remaining background strips, subcut (16) 2½" squares from each for a **total of (112)** 2½" background squares. Set the background squares aside for the wonky star blocks.

2 make summer in the park blocks

Take the 32 print strips set aside earlier for the Summer in the Park blocks. Choose 2 strips and sew them together lengthwise. Press the seam allowance toward the darker print. **Make 16** strip sets. **2A**

Place 1 strip set atop another strip set with right sides facing. Make a tube by sewing the 2 long edges of the strip sets together using a ¼" seam allowance. **Make 8** tubes. **2B**

Lay 1 tube horizontally on your cutting surface. Lay the trimmer on top, lining up the long edge of the trimmer with the bottom edge of the tube. Carefully cut the top 2 sides along the edge of the trimmer. **2C**

Rotate the trimmer so that the long edge of the trimmer is now at the top of the tube. Line up the top and diagonal edges of the trimmer and tube. Carefully cut the diagonal along the edge of the trimmer. **2D**

Continue rotating and cutting using the trimmer to cut 8 strip squares from each tube for a **total of 64** strip squares. Open and press the seam allowances of each strip square toward the darker fabric. **2E**

Arrange 4 strip squares into a 4-patch formation as shown. Sew the units together in rows. **2F**

Press the seams of the top row to the left and the bottom row to the right. Nest the seams and sew the rows together to complete the block. **Make 16** blocks. **2G**

Block Size: 11" finished

3 make wonky stars

Select (14) 2½" print squares to use in the center of the stars and (56) 2½" background squares and set them aside for the moment. Use the remaining 2½" squares to make the star legs.

47

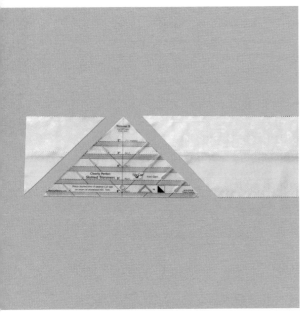

1 Lay 1 tube horizontally on your cutting surface. Lay the trimmer on top as shown. Carefully cut the top 2 sides along the edge of the trimmer.

2 Continue rotating and cutting using the trimmer to cut 8 strip squares from each tube. Open and press the seam allowances of each strip square toward the darker fabric.

3 Arrange 4 strip squares into a 4-patch formation as shown. Sew the units together in rows. Nest the seams and sew the rows together to complete the block.

4 Place a 2½" print square on an angle atop a 2½" background square with right sides facing. Sew ¼" in from the angled edge of the print square. Press the print piece over the seam allowance. Turn the unit over and use the background square as a guide to trim the print fabric.

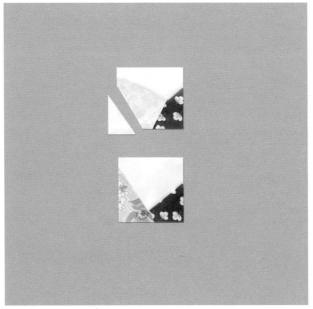

5 Repeat the steps to sew, press, and trim another angled square to create an additional star leg. Make 4 star leg squares.

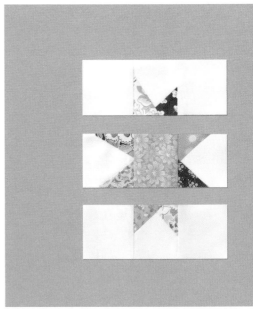

6 Sew a background square to either side of a star leg square. Make 2. Sew a star leg square to either side of each print square you set aside earlier. Nest the seams and sew the rows together to complete the block.

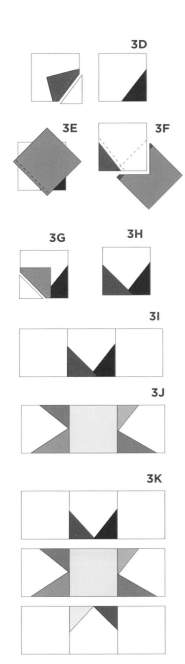

3D

3E   3F

3G   3H

3I

3J

3K

Place a 2½″ print square on an angle (any angle) atop a 2½″ background square with right sides facing. Make sure your print square is placed a little past the halfway point. Sew ¼″ in from the angled edge of the print square. **3A**

Press the piece flat to set the seam, then press the print piece over the seam allowance. **3B**

Turn the unit over and use the background square as a guide to trim the print fabric so that all of the edges are even. Save the trimmed scrap to use for another leg of the star. (You should be able to make at least 2 star legs from each print square.) **3C**

Turn the unit back over so that the right side of the fabric is facing up. Fold the print fabric of the star leg back to reveal the seam allowance and trim the excess background fabric ¼″ away from the sewn seam. Fold the star leg back so the right side of the fabric is facing up and press. **3D**

Place another print square or a trimmed print scrap on the adjacent side of the square. Make sure the edge of the second print piece crosses over the first star leg by at least ¼″. Stitch ¼″ in from the edge of the print piece. **3E**

Press the print piece over the seam allowance. Turn the unit over and use the background square as a guide to trim the print fabric so all of the edges are even. Notice your square is still 2½″. **3F**

Turn the unit back over so that the right side of the fabric is facing up. Fold the print fabric of the star leg back to reveal the seam allowance and trim the excess fabric ¼″ away from the sewn seam. **3G**

Fold the star leg back so the right side of the fabric is facing up and press. **Make 56** star leg squares. **Note:** Have fun with this and don't try to make all of the star legs alike! **3H**

Sew a background square to either side of a star leg square. Press the seams towards the background squares. **Make 28. 3I**

Sew a star leg square to either side of each print square you set aside earlier. Make sure the star legs point away from the center square. Press the seams toward the center square. **Make 14. 3J**

Nest the seams and sew the rows together to complete the block. **Make 14** blocks. **3K**

Block Size: 6″ finished

4 arrange & sew

Arrange 7 wonky star blocks side by side and sew the blocks together in a row. **4A**

Sew a 1½″ x 6½″ background rectangle set aside earlier to each end to complete the row. **Make 2** wonky star rows. **4B**

Arrange 4 Summer in the Park blocks side by side and sew the blocks together to make a row. **Make 4** Summer in the Park rows. **4C**

Lay out the quilt center as shown in the diagram on page 51. Rows 1, 3, 4 and 6 are Summer in the Park rows and rows 2 and 5 are wonky star rows. Press the seam allowances of all the odd-numbered rows to the left and all the even-numbered rows to the right. Nest the seams and sew the rows together.

5 inner border

Taking the (6) 2½" background strips set aside earlier, sew the strips end-to-end to make 1 long strip.

Refer to Borders (pg. 102) in the Construction Basics to measure and cut the inner borders. The strips are approximately 56½" for the sides and approximately 48½" for the top and bottom.

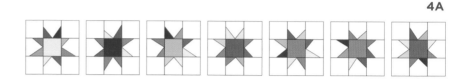

4A

6 outer border

Cut (7) 6½" strips across the width of the fabric. Sew the strips together end-to-end to make 1 long strip. Trim the borders from this strip.

Refer to Borders (pg. 102) in the Construction Basics to measure and cut the outer borders. The strips are approximately 60½" for each side, top and bottom.

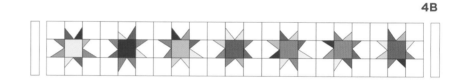

4B

7 quilt & bind

Layer the quilt with batting and backing and quilt. After the quilting is complete, square up the quilt and trim away all excess batting and backing. Add binding to complete the quilt. See Construction Basics (pg. 102) for binding instructions.

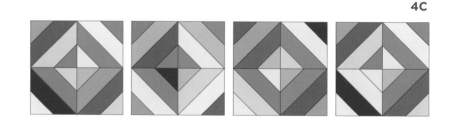

4C

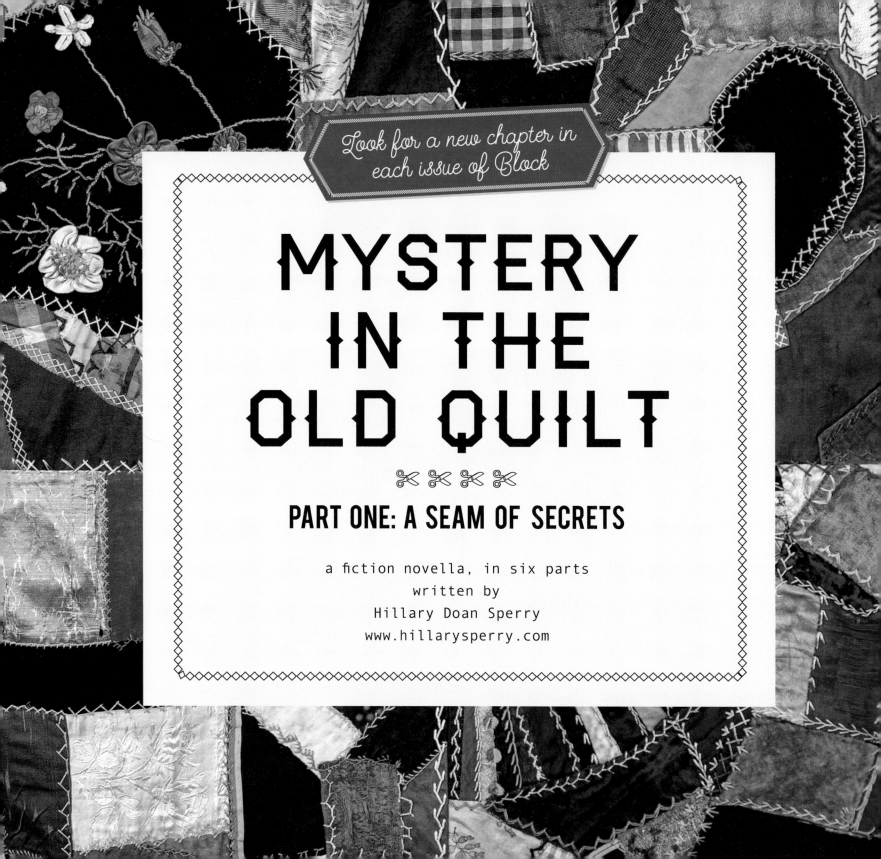

Look for a new chapter in
each issue of Block

MYSTERY IN THE OLD QUILT

✄ ✄ ✄ ✄

PART ONE: A SEAM OF SECRETS

a fiction novella, in six parts
written by
Hillary Doan Sperry
www.hillarysperry.com

The clock seemed to tick louder the faster she moved. Jenny checked her hair and pulled on a sweater. The new strip quilt she'd been working on sat abandoned on the table. She'd have to finish it later. If she didn't hurry she'd be late for the presentation.

Ron folded the beautiful quilt the local guild had prepared and handed it to Jenny on her way out the door. Over twenty women sent in blocks and more had helped with the stitching. She and Bernadette sat with sewing needles earlier that afternoon tacking the blue floral binding in place.

Jenny took the quilt and pecked a kiss to Ron's cheek, "I'll see you soon."

He smiled and a wrinkle creased from the corner of his eye. Jenny reached up, holding his face for a moment.

"I love you, sweetheart," he told her and spun her away toward the door, "But you have got to go!"

Jenny chuckled as she moved to the car. She waved goodbye and drove the few blocks to the old church. The sun was on its way down as she pulled into the parking lot.

Light glinted off the beveled windows. Jenny waved to several women on her way across the gravel parking lot, grateful that she was part of a community that cared enough to pull together when someone needed them.

A redbud tree hung across the sidewalk, bright pink blossoms popping out along every branch, like someone had piped frosting in the trees. Jenny stepped onto the sidewalk as her friend, Bernadette, shut her car door. Bernie's sister Dotty waved, and the two joined Jenny.

"Oh my, but that's a beautiful quilt." Dotty winked giving the blue pinwheels a pat.

"Well, the binding is fantastic anyway," Bernie added and gave the fabric a second look, "Wait, is that my side or yours?"

Jenny laughed, "Does it matter?"

Bernie hesitated, shooting a grin at the two women, "Not sure I should answer that."

Dotty's laughter surrounded them as the three women climbed the steps to the front door of the clapboard building. Loretta, the president of the Hamilton Quilt Guild, stood at the door greeting guests with a perpetual frown on her face. Jenny smiled brightly determined that one of these days she'd get her to smile back.

"Welcome," Loretta's frown deepened at Jenny's approach. "I'll take that," she said removing the quilt from Jenny's arms. "I was starting to worry you wouldn't make it."

Jenny tipped her head, "You can count on me. It was a joy to help, Lo."

Loretta harrumphed, "That's good because Blair's already here, and it would have been a shame to send her away empty-handed."

"I wouldn't do that to you." Jenny squeezed Loretta's elbow as she and Dotty stepped past. Bernie had saved them a seat toward the back of the crowded room. Jenny gave a soft whistle, "I haven't seen the meeting this full in months."

Loretta moved to the front of the room. The door opened behind her and a straggler slid into the last of the open seats, right next to Jenny.

There was a loud, uh-hem as Loretta cleared her throat. "I'd like to welcome everyone to our monthly guild meeting. Before we have the show-and-tell portion of our meeting, I need to mention our special guest.

"This will be a particularly poignant meeting for me and many of you, I imagine. Tonight we have Gina Sloane's daughter, Blair, joining us. Gina passed away only a few weeks ago and the quilt we were preparing for Gina while she was sick will now go to her only daughter.

"Losing Gina was a blow to each of us ..." Loretta rambled on about Gina and how wonderful she was.

Jenny glanced at Blair. The poor girl watched the carpet, her face buried in strawberry blond hair. Loretta's 'memorial' seemed to be hitting her hard.

"Just give her the quilt, Lo!" Bernie called. Blair's head lifted and a shaky smile pulled at the corner of her lips. Women chuckled, but Loretta glared in Bernie's direction before going on.

"Here, Blair. If you'll come up, by me." Loretta gestured to her side. When she finally handed over the quilt, relief poured over the young woman. Her chest heaved in a deep breath, she lifted her head to look at the crowd. Blair only managed a few words, then made a beeline across the crowd. She slowed at the back of the room. The dark-haired woman beside Jenny stood, vacating her seat.

"Blair," she whispered and pointed to the chair, "come sit."

Blair hesitated but slid into the open space with a muffled, "Thank you."

Jenny patted Blair's knee, sliding an arm around her shoulder. "How are you holding up?"

"I'm fine." Blair sighed and shook her head. "Actually, it's been a little rocky."

"I can imagine." Jenny let Blair take the lead on the conversation.

The women around them broke into applause as people displayed projects for the show-and-tell part of the evening. Blair's shoulders relaxed with the burst of noise. She scooted closer to Jenny and said, "I actually have a question for you."

"For me?" Jenny tried not to show her surprise.

Blair was a friend, but that was mostly because of her mother, Gina.

"Well, my mother was working on a quilt. It's been in our family for generations. It's got embroidery all over it tracking family lines. Kind of like a family history, or a family tree."

"That sounds amazing."

"It could be, but it's kind of a mess. Half the seams are coming undone. My mother finished the embroidery, but I don't know how to finish piecing the top." Blair's eyes teared up. "I know you're busy, but I don't know who else to ask."

Jenny took Blair's hands in her own. "Don't worry. We'll take care of it. I have a trip a few days from now, but I'm happy to help. Do you want to bring it by later and I'll start when I return?"

"That might be too late." Blair looked at her lap. "Finishing the quilt is one of the conditions of my mother's will. I have to finish it within a month of her death, or the insurance money goes to charity. I don't care about that, but I'm supposed to get a letter from my mom as well. But only if I finish it in time."

"Oh." Jenny thought through the time-frame and Blair's head drooped. "Within a month? That's only five days, and I leave in four." Blair started to shake her head, but Jenny stopped her. "That's still four days to put a half-finished quilt together. It's not a problem."

Blair's brow wrinkled. "There's more. There's a secret in the quilt. For it to be considered finished, we have to repair it and solve the mystery."

"What's the secret?"

"I don't know. All I have is a note the lawyer gave me with the quilt."

"What's it say?"

"Not much." Blair reached into her purse and pulled out a piece of paper not much larger than a sticky note: 'Look inside, or I'll be gone forever.'

"That's ominous," Dotty said, leaning over Jenny's shoulder. Applause sounded again and Bernie stood.

Scooting past the women, a large bundle in her hands, Bernie paused at the end of the row. "My turn to show off. Oh, and I'll help if you want." Blair's reluctant smile spoke of relief.

It was all Jenny needed to know. She'd finish the quilt for Blair. "Just tell me what needs to be done."

⚞ ⚟ ⚞

When Jenny arrived at her studio the next morning, Blair was sitting on the front steps with a quilt piled in her lap. Jenny hurried up the steps and hugged the girl. "Is this the quilt?"

Blair nodded opening a few of the folds.

"Blair, this is a family treasure." Jenny shook out the quilt. Rows of eight-pointed stars interlocked with pieced and embroidered half-square triangles. Names and dates were stitched in what Jenny assumed were family groupings.

Jenny's new assistant walked up, "Is everyone alright? Are we stuck out here?"

"We're fine." Jenny folded the quilt and gestured for them to go inside. "Oh Blair, this is my new assistant Michelle Peters. Michelle, this is Blair Sloane."

"It's nice to meet you." Michelle nodded at Blair and moved to the door.

Blair held out her hand. "You probably don't remember me, but we were in high school together. I was a couple years behind you."

"Oh how funny! You know, I think I do remember."

With a wave of her hand, Blair brushed the history aside, "It's nice to see you again. And thank you, Jenny, for working on the quilt. I can meet whenever you think it will be ready."

Jenny winked at her, "Then I'll see you tomorrow. It's in much better shape than I thought."

"Tomorrow, then."

✂ ✂ ✂

For the next several hours Jenny dissected the old quilt. Reassembling pieces that had come apart and recreating block settings when necessary. The pieces went back together nicely, the whole quilt requiring less work than she'd anticipated. However, something still nagged at her mind.

Jenny had been over the entire thing, stitch by stitch, and she couldn't figure out what the mystery might be. It was just an old quilt.

She held up a block section. The piece would separate two embroidered blocks. Spotting the safety pin she'd marked the original block with, Jenny started unstitching the connecting seams.

A piece of the star's point began to separate, and she groaned in frustration. Lifting the little red triangle, Jenny tried to finger press the corner into place. She tugged at the fabric surprised to find it was double layered.

The extra layer of fabric had been appliquéd carefully on top of a corner star. Jenny ran a finger between the fabric layers, making sure she wasn't going to compromise the construction of the quilt if she took it apart. A thrill ran through her. Something was there. A spark lit inside her and she wondered if she had found what Blair had been looking for.

Jenny pulled her thread scissors out, tempted to clip away the excess fabric. She ended up unstitching the whole side in an effort to retain as much of the vintage material as possible.

When the appliqué fell away, Jenny could hardly believe what it had been hiding:

Delicate handwork etched tiny flowers and ribbons across the cream fabric. The artwork surrounded a short line of prose and dates.

"Michelle! Come look at this." Jenny wished Blair had returned.

Her assistant joined her at the worktable. Jenny brushed a hand over the sweet embroidery, "It's so different from any of the other blocks."

10-01-1974
Love anew has come to me.
Love again I must set free.
10-09-1974

"It's ... lovely?" Michelle sounded unimpressed.

A tap sounded near the front door. Jenny looked around. "Why is someone knocking? No one knocks here."

Michelle's eyebrows lifted and she jumped again. "My mother! I forgot to tell you. She's stopping by. Is that okay? She works with Missouri Star part-time and wanted to swing by before heading to her other job. You don't mind do you?"

"Two jobs? Oh, that's challenging." Compassion rose in Jenny's chest for the hardworking woman.

Michelle nodded. "Yes. She's always worked two, but now that my dad's starting a business it's especially important."

"Of course, of course. Go let her in. Maybe she can take a look at this block with us."

Michelle shot the embroidered quilt block another glance and rushed to the door.

The woman's tall figure and dark hair were strikingly different from her daughter's. She greeted Michelle, leaning against her desk and Jenny felt a flash of recognition. "You sat by me at the guild meeting yesterday."

The woman smiled. "You're right. My name is Claudia."

Michelle put an arm around her mother and pointed to the table. "So, do you think that's the mystery?"

"I don't know for sure. It's different though." Jenny turned away from Claudia and looked back to the quilt.

"It's just a poem," Claudia said, studying the fabric. "What's so mysterious about that?"

Jenny indicated several of the family group names around it. "Nowhere else has this kind of work or detail. Just names and dates in the other blocks."

Jenny puzzled over the words, picking up a spool of thread and spinning it in her hand. "Love again I must set free."

Claudia coughed. "Maybe someone died?"

"Maybe," Jenny answered. *But who? A spouse? A child?* The block was set right next to the one Gina had created for their family, but the time frame didn't line up right. According to the quilt, Gina and her husband Frank hadn't even married until a year after the poem's date.

"Could Gina have been married before?" Michelle asked.

Claudia answered before Jenny had a chance,

"I have no idea. She and Frank were pretty steady in high school."

Jenny gave the quiet woman a long look. "Were you in school with Gina?"

"I was a senior that year. Which would have made her a junior, I think. I didn't know her well. She mostly hung out with Frank."

"Really? No girlfriends to hang out with? No other relationships?" Jenny was surprised. Gina had always seemed so social.

Claudia shrugged. "Not really."

Jenny watched her walk away an odd feeling in her gut that she couldn't take their conversation at face value.

She turned back to the quilt and ran a finger over the block again. Love had changed Gina thirty years before. And according to her note, if they didn't figure it out, they would lose Gina again.

"Well," Jenny looked at her friends gathered in the studio, "It looks like we have a mystery on our hands."

to be continued next issue ...

<<<>>>

JENNY'S JOURNAL

In this quilting journal, I want to give you a glimpse into my personal sewing projects. Although I film many quilting tutorials—at least one every week—I still feel the need to create on my own time. It helps feed my soul to spend some quiet time in my studio and sew without a deadline or a to-do list. This sewing is simply for pleasure!

You might wonder what personal projects I've got in progress, what quilts I've recently finished, what plans I have for quilts in 2020, and what excites me lately. I keep a simple record of what I've been working on recently. Sometimes it's a fun scrappy project I started during my 15 minutes of play or it's a gift for a family member. Often, it's all about a fabric line that caught my eye and I just had to make something with it. Whatever strikes my fancy, you'll find it right here.

Love,

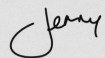

Here are some of my journals I've kept through the years.

You may have noticed this pattern elsewhere in BLOCK. It's a version of the Summer Stars quilt in cool blue and white prints for my grandson, Isaac, and his wife, Aislinn. It was made with the classic Blue Byrd collection by Williamsburg for Windham Fabrics. It reminds me of the patterns found on Dutch delftware pottery. I wanted to make them a gift they would cherish for a lifetime. My hope is this timeless pattern and color palette will always look fresh, no matter what the current trend may be. I always enjoy creating quilts as gifts and there is love stitched into every quilt I make.

Celebrate Sewing
Made by Jenny Doan
Finished December 2019

I fell in love with Riley Blake's "Celebrate Sewing" quilt the very first time I saw it! I thought it was so cute with blocks featuring pieced scissors, sewing machines, spools of thread, and seam rippers. I don't often make quilts for myself so, this was a fun exception. I made it during a sewing retreat this winter and it was such a treat to piece together. A couple of times a year, I take a day to sew something just for myself. Sometimes it's an easy project and sometimes I want to challenge and stretch myself with a more advanced project. This quilt was right in that sweet spot, not too difficult, but not too basic either. It was an absolute pleasure to create. I felt like it spoke to my heart about so many of the things I love. I plan to hang it up in my sewing studio and look at it every time I'm there!

HAVE YOU GOT A MINUTE?

5 MINUTES

I have a complicated relationship with to-do lists. It almost seems like once I put something on my to-do list it becomes a chore. Well, let's banish that thought! Instead of the dreaded to-do list, what about another type of list? I like to keep a gratitude journal that I try to write in for five minutes a day. I reflect on all the good things that happened and jot them down before bed. It helps me focus on positive outcomes and rest easier.

5 HOURS

When you have a spare afternoon or a lazy weekend ahead of you, take a few hours to really assess the quilt projects you have planned or have already started. Sort them into stacks starting with those that only need a few finishing touches all the way down to those you haven't even started piecing yet. Put them in order according to priority. When you get a little time during the week, you can simply pull out a project and get a bit of it done. You'll be finished before you know it!

5 DAYS

Now, I know five days sounds like a lot, but it doesn't have to happen all at once. Slowly, take the time to write down a memory. Expand from a list and start filling in details or adding photos. You'll be surprised at how much you remember once you get started! Then, if you'd like to share what you've written, email your quilting story to us at **blockstories@missouriquiltco.com.** We can't wait to read it!

Use the layout on the opposite page to explore these fun prompts.

5 MINUTE PROMPT:
- What made you smile today?
- What did you do for fun today?
- What interesting new skill did you learn or discover that you want to try?

5 HOUR PROMPT:
- Make a list of all the UFOs you have and decide if any have potential for a project.
- Sort and organize your fabric stash.
- Plan out your next project!

5 DAY PROMPT:
- Start a quilt journal to keep track of all the quilts you make or give away.
- Begin a new project you've been wanting to get to but haven't had the time.

Quilting in Color
Window Box Quilt

Kona Cotton really "gets" me. My love for color runs deep, and Kona offers 365 different shades. Three hundred and sixty-five, that's one for every day of the year!

After all, quilters don't quilt with "pink." We use watermelon and peony and bubble gum and primrose. And when we want to match a stack of pretty prints exactly, we can't pick up any old blue! We have to scan through peacock and sea glass and waterfall to find the perfect hue.

Kona made it easy by creating a color card decked out with little one-inch fabric swatches of each and every color available, so you can quickly find the best matches for your fabric. It may seem silly, but I absolutely love drinking in all those gorgeous colors. I try to pick a favorite, but I just can't!

Best of all, every year Kona releases a limited-edition Color of the Year. In 2016, it was an electrifying yellow called "Highlight." In 2017, it was a coral pink called "Flamingo." "Tiger Lily," a bold red-orange, took the stage in 2018, followed by a playful aqua called "Splash" in 2019.

The Kona Color of the Year is available in yardage and precuts, and Kona provides wonderful patterns and project ideas to best suit the shade. But, at the end of the year, the color is retired. It really is a "get it before it's gone" situation.

Leading up to the announcement of the 2020 Color of the Year, there was plenty of speculation. Quilters guessed everything from metallic gold to indigo, but Robert Kaufman Fabrics was tight-lipped until the week before Christmas.

Finally, "Enchanted" was debuted, and we all let out a collective gasp of delight. It's so rich! It's so elegant! It's so full of possibilities!

Here at Missouri Star, we jumped right in, designing new quilts with this beguiling shade of green. With just a whisper of blue, Enchanted looks fantastic paired with just about anything!

So go ahead, let your imagination run wild before this gorgeous green is retired and 2021 brings us a brand new Color of the Year!

Check out Kona's color of the year, Enchanted by Robert Kaufman Fabrics at www.robertkaufman.com

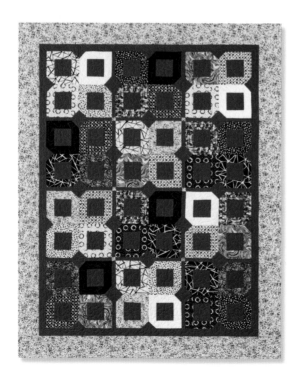

materials

QUILT SIZE
68" x 86"

BLOCK SIZE
17" finished

QUILT TOP
1 roll 2½" print strips*
2¼ yards background fabric
   - includes sashing and inner border**

OUTER BORDER
1½ yards

BINDING
¾ yard

BACKING
5¼ yards - vertical seam(s)
   or 2¾ yards 108" wide

*__Note:__ *Your print strips must have at least 42" of usable width and have at least 8 pairs of matching strips.*

**__Note:__ *2 packages of 5" background squares and 1 yard of matching background fabric can be substituted.*

SAMPLE QUILT
Pen and Ink by Studio RK for Robert Kaufman Fabrics
Enchanted Kona Color of the Year 2020 by Robert Kaufman Fabrics

2A

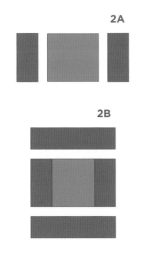

2B

3A **3B**

3C **3D**

4A

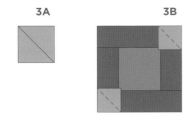

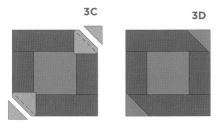

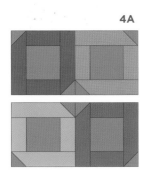

1 sort & cut

Select 4 matching pairs of 2½" light print strips and 4 matching pairs of 2½" dark print strips. From each strip cut:

- (3) 2½" x 5" rectangles
- (3) 2½" x 9" rectangles

From each of the remaining (24) 2½" print strips, cut:

- (2) 2½" x 5" rectangles
- (2) 2½" x 9" rectangles

Keep the rectangles in matching sets of (2) 2½" x 5" rectangles and (2) 2½" x 9" rectangles, for a **total of 48** sets.

From the remaining pieces of print strips, cut (6) 1½" squares and set them aside for cornerstones.

Note: You may choose to have cornerstones cut from different print strips, or all from the same strip as we have done on our quilt.

From the background fabric, cut (9) 5" strips across the width of the fabric. Subcut each strip into (8) 5" squares for a **total of (72)** 5" background squares.

Select (24) 5" squares and cut them in half vertically and horizontally to create (4) 2½" squares from each, for a **total of (96)** 2½" background squares. Set these aside for the moment. Set the remaining background fabric aside for the sashing and inner border.

2 make box units

Taking 1 set of print rectangles, sew a 2½" x 5" rectangle to both sides of a 5" background square using a ¼" seam allowance. Press the seams toward the darker fabric. **2A**

Sew a 2½" x 9" rectangle to the top and bottom of the unit and press the seams toward the darker fabric. **2B**

Repeat sewing rectangles to the sides, top and bottom of each 5" background square for a **total of 48** box units.

3 make snowball units

Draw a diagonal line corner to corner on the wrong side of each 2½" background square. **3A**

To snowball the box units made earlier, lay a marked background square atop the 2 corners of 1 unit as shown with right sides facing. Sew on the diagonal lines. Cut the excess fabric ¼" away from the sewn seams. **3B 3C**

Press toward the snowballed corners. Repeat snowballing corners on each box unit. **3D**

4 block construction

Sort the snowballed units into 24 light units and 24 dark units.

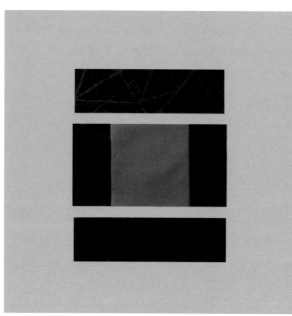

1 Taking 1 set of print rectangles, sew a 2½" x 5" rectangle to both sides of a 5" background square using a ¼" seam allowance. Press the seams toward the darker fabric.

2 Sew a 2½" x 9" rectangle to the top and bottom of the unit and press the seams toward the darker fabric. Repeat sewing rectangles to the sides, top and bottom of each 5" background square for a total of 48 box units.

3 To snowball the box units, lay a marked background square atop the 2 corners of 1 unit as shown with right sides facing. Sew on the diagonal lines. Cut the excess fabric ¼" away from the sewn seams.

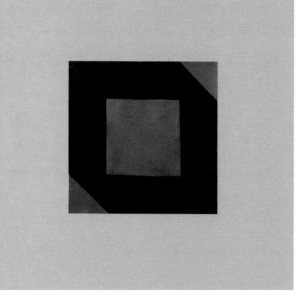

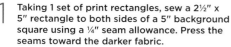

4 Press toward the snowballed corners. Repeat snowballing 2 opposite corners on each box unit.

5 Select 4 dark units and arrange them into a 4-patch formation as shown, making note of the orientation of the units when laying out your block. Sew the units together in rows. Press the seams of the top row to the left and the bottom row to the right.

6 Nest the seams and sew the rows together to complete the block. Make 6 dark blocks. Repeat arranging and sewing of light snowballed units to make 6 light blocks.

Select 4 dark units and arrange them into a 4-patch formation as shown, making note of the orientation of the units when laying out your block. Sew the units together in rows. **4A**

Press the seams of the top row to the left and the bottom row to the right. Nest the seams and sew the rows together to complete the block. **Make 6** dark blocks. **4B**

Repeat arranging and sewing of light snowballed units to **make 6** light blocks. **4C**

Block Size: 17" finished

5 make horizontal sashing strips

From the background fabric, cut (9) 1½" strips across the width of the fabric. Subcut each strip into 1½" x 17½" sashing rectangles. Each strip will yield 2 rectangles and a **total of 17** are needed.

Sew a 1½" x 17½" rectangle to either side of a 1½" print square. Add a 1½" print square and end the row with another 1½" x 17½" rectangle. Press the seams toward the background rectangles. **Make 3. 5A**

4B

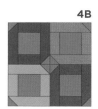

4C

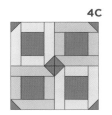

5A

6 arrange & sew

Refer to the diagram below as needed to lay out the blocks in **4 rows** with each row being made up of **3 blocks.** Each row has alternating dark and light blocks. As you make each row, sew a 1½" x 17½" sashing rectangle between each block. Press the seam allowances toward the sashing rectangles.

Sew the rows together adding a horizontal sashing strip between each row to complete the quilt center. Press the seam allowances toward the sashing strips.

7 inner border

From the background fabric, cut (7) 2½" strips across the width of fabric. Sew the strips end-to-end to make 1 long strip. Trim the borders from this strip.

Refer to Borders (pg. 102) in the Construction Basics to measure and cut the inner borders. The strips are approximately 71½" for the sides and approximately 57½" for the top and bottom.

8 outer border

Cut (8) 6" strips across the width of the fabric. Sew the strips together end-to-end to make 1 long strip. Trim the borders from this strip.

Refer to Borders (pg. 102) in the Construction Basics to measure and cut the outer borders. The strips are approximately 75½" for the sides and approximately 68½" for the top and bottom.

9 quilt & bind

Layer the quilt with batting and backing and quilt. After the quilting is complete, square up the quilt and trim away all excess batting and backing. Add binding to complete the quilt. See Construction Basics (pg. 102) for binding instructions.

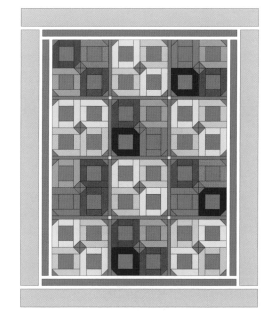

Oh, How Times Have Changed!
Heart to Heart Table Runner

Two hundred years ago, quilters sewed every stitch by hand. Now, our home sewing machines can complete seam after seam at incredible speed. (And the electric seam ripper can undo those seams just as quickly. Just in case...) Modern computerized embroidery machines and longarm quilting machines fill entire quilt tops with breathtakingly intricate designs—all with the touch of a button. Oh, how times have changed!

Fifty years ago, we fashioned templates out of cardboard and used fabric shears to cut five-inch squares out of a sea of yardage. Now, rotary cutters, self-healing mats, and plastic templates make quick work of cutting. Die cut machines crank out perfect shapes one after another, and precut prefused appliqué pieces come completely ready for action! So much effort is saved on the prep work, we can spend more time actually quilting!

Twenty years ago, we wandered shop aisles, trying to coordinate fabric. Would a yard of each be enough? Or too much? It was always so tricky to guess! Now, we can order a pack of perfectly-portioned precuts and know the colors and prints will harmonize like a heavenly choir! And we don't have to race from store to store in order to find what we need. The internet allows us to shop from the comfort of home any hour of the day, even when creative ideas crop up in the middle of the night.

Ten years ago, we learned to quilt locally. And if there wasn't a knowledgeable friend or community class nearby, chances are we didn't learn to quilt at all. Now, the internet is bursting with excellent instruction. A quick search will uncover tutorials on every topic from the first cut of fabric to the final binding stitch.

Friends, we have reached the golden age of quilting! We have access to wonderful supplies, brilliant technology, and limitless information. Best of all, we have the ability to connect with quilters around the globe.

We use Facebook, Instagram, and YouTube to learn and laugh with hundreds of thousands of our best friends. Tips and encouragement are shared liberally on the Missouri Star online forum. And at our Quiltsby.me website, quilters show off their latest creations and the stories behind them.

Through the magic of the internet, we are like one massive quilt guild. People from all walks of life are brought together by a love of quilting. If I had to pick a favorite aspect of quilting in 2020, that would be it. The community. Oh, how I adore the friendships and the feeling of belonging, even across oceans. It truly is a treasure to feel connected to so many wonderful people.

And while tools and techniques constantly evolve, one thing will never change: the desire to create. Quilting ignites something in the soul. Stitched by hand or stitched by computer, it's all the same. Our great-great-grandparents felt it, and our great-great-grandchildren will, too.

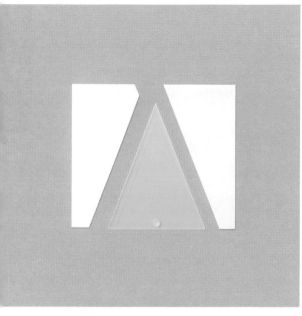

1 Carefully trim all the way along the right side of the template. Move the right side triangle you just cut out of the way and trim along the left side of the template.

2 Lay a background wedge, wrong side up, on top of the left side triangle as shown. Sew along the right edge using a ¼" seam allowance. Open and press toward the darker fabric.

3 Lay the right side print triangle on top of the pieced unit, right sides together, and lining up the right edges as shown. Sew along the right edge using a ¼" seam allowance.

4 Open and press the seam allowance toward the darker fabric. Repeat sewing background wedges and print triangle sets to make a total of 164 of Unit A.

5 Trim each unit to 4" square by trimming the top first, leaving ½" above the point of the wedge. Trim the bottom as needed. Measure 2" from both sides of the wedge point and trim either side as needed.

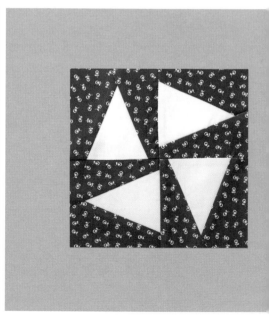

6 Arrange 4 of Unit A into a 4-patch formation as shown. Sew the units together in rows. Nest the seams and sew the rows together to complete the block.

materials

PROJECT SIZE
46" x 13"

BLOCK SIZE
9" finished

PROJECT TOP
1 package 5" print squares
2 coordinating 5"
   light print squares
   or ¼ yard of light print

BINDING
½ yard

BACKING
¾ yard - cut parallel to the
   selvages and sewn together
   along the short ends

SAMPLE QUILT
Bramble Cottage by Brenda Riddle Designs
for Moda Fabrics

2A

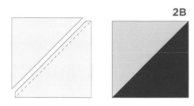

2B

3A

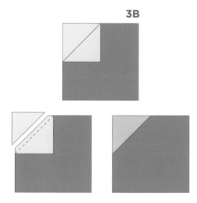

3B

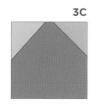

3C

1 sort & cut

Separate your package of 5″ squares into 11 lights, 15 mediums and 16 darks. Add the additional 5″ light squares to the stack of light squares. If you chose to use yardage instead of precut squares, see the note below for cutting. Set the stacks aside for the moment.

Note: From the light print yardage, cut a 5″ strip across the width of the fabric. Subcut (2) 5″ squares from the strip and place them with your stack of light print squares. Set the remaining light print fabric aside for another project.

Cut each of the light squares in half. Each square will yield (2) 2½″ x 5″ rectangles and a **total of 26** are needed.

Select 8 medium squares and set them aside for now. Cut the 7 remaining squares in half vertically and horizontally. Each 5″ square will yield (4) 2½″ squares and a **total of 26** squares are needed.

Set the stack of dark squares aside for now.

2 make half-square triangles

Pick up the 8 medium squares you set aside earlier. Mark a diagonal line on the reverse side of the squares once corner to corner. **2A**

Select a dark square you set aside earlier. Lay a marked medium square on top of your dark square with right sides facing

and sew them together on the marked line. Trim the excess fabric ¼″ away from the sewn seam. Open to reveal a half-square triangle and press the seam allowance towards the darker fabric. **Make 8** half-square triangle units. **2B**

3 snowball corners

Pick up 16 of the 2½″ medium squares and mark a diagonal line on the reverse side of the squares once corner to corner. **3A**

Select a 5″ dark square and place a marked square on 1 corner as shown. Sew along the marked line and trim the excess fabric ¼″ away from the sewn seam. Open to reveal a snowballed corner. Press the seam allowance towards the snowballed corner. **3B**

Repeat to snowball an adjacent corner of the 5″ square. **Make 8** snowballed units. **3C**

4 block construction

Select 2 half-square triangle units and 2 snowballed units. Arrange the units into a 4-patch formation as shown. **4A**

Sew the units together in pairs to form rows. Press the seam allowance of the upper row to the right and the lower row to the left. **4B**

Nest the seams and sew the 2 rows together to complete the block. **Make 4** blocks. **4C**

Block Size: 9″ finished

 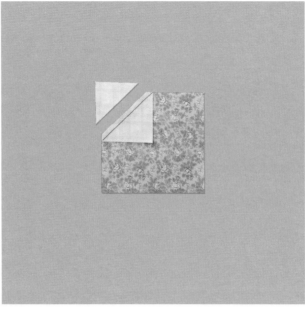 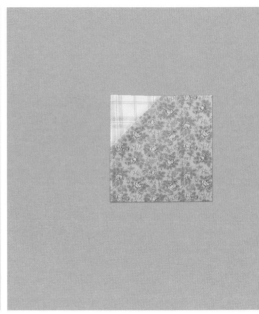

1 Lay a marked medium square on top of your dark square with right sides facing and sew on the marked line. Trim the excess fabric ¼" away from the sewn seam. Open to reveal a half-square triangle. Make 8 half-square triangles.

2 Select a 5" dark square and place a marked square on 1 corner as shown. Sew along the marked line and trim the excess fabric ¼" away from the sewn seam.

3 Open to reveal a snowballed corner. Press the seam allowance towards the snowballed corner.

 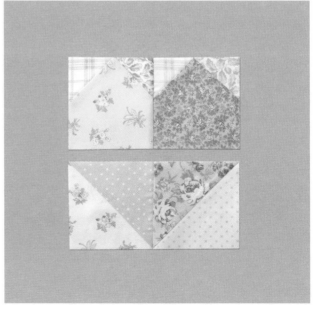

4 Repeat to snowball an adjacent corner of the 5" square. Make 8 snowballed units.

5 Arrange the units into a 4-patch formation as shown. Sew the units together in pairs to form rows. Nest the seams and sew the 2 rows together to complete the block. Make 4 blocks.

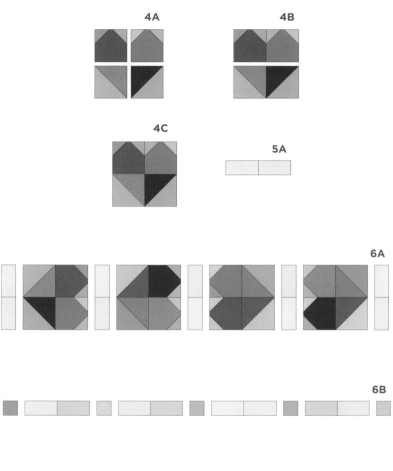

4A

4B

4C

5A

6A

6B

5 make sashing strips

Select (2) 2½" x 5" light rectangles and sew them together end-to-end. Press the seam to 1 side to make a sashing strip. **Make 13** sashing strips. **5A**

6 arrange & sew

Lay out the blocks in a row as shown. Place a sashing strip at each end of the row and between each of the blocks. Sew the heart row together. Press the seams toward the right. **6A**

Arrange 4 sashing strips in a row as shown. Place a 2½" medium print square at each end of the row and between each of the strips. Sew the sashing row together. Press the seams toward the left. **Make 2. 6B**

Lay out the table runner as shown in the diagram below. The heart row will be centered between the 2 sashing rows. Nest the seams and sew the rows together to complete the project top.

7 quilt & bind

Layer the table runner with batting and backing and quilt. After the quilting is complete, square up the table runner and trim away all excess batting and backing. Add binding to complete the project. See Construction Basics (pg. 102) for binding instructions.

The Gift of Comfort and Love
Hopscotch Quilt

When I was in school it seemed like those long days of reading, writing, and arithmetic would never end. I loved learning, but I couldn't wait to get outside and play! I was a daydreamer and my teacher constantly caught me staring out the window with my hand on my chin, wishing I were out at recess running around, skipping rope, and playing hopscotch with my friends. Those days are long gone and I can't help but sympathize with my teachers now. They all tried so hard to keep our attention! I'll always be grateful to my teachers and their tireless efforts. One teacher, Tonya Sherman, sent me her story of how she started quilting. She was gifted a quilt by one of her students and it changed her life.

"I have been a teacher for over twenty years. I never thought of myself as creative at all! A few years back, I was given a quilt at the end of the year by a very generous parent. At the time I thought, 'what a nice gift', never realizing the super healing powers it had. I found myself cuddling under it every morning with my cup of coffee. Then, my son began to use it. Then, whenever someone got off the couch, the next person would take it! It soon became the 'hot commodity' in the house.

"The next year, that same parent's twin girls were in my class and, after sending this parent a few photos of my family hogging MY quilt, she decided to make me another one, but in super 'girly' fabrics. Surely it would scare off the boys from using it. Not a chance! Even when my 15-year-old son had a sleepover with the guys, he used my super girly quilt to camp out with his friends.

"That summer my husband became ill and needed a series of surgeries. After long days in the hospital waiting room and ER visits, I would take a hot shower and cuddle up with the quilt, and it gave me such comfort during this time. I thought, how wonderful it must be to have such a talent and to be able to give someone this kind of comfort and love.

"When my niece decided to get married, I knew I wanted to give her something special, and I decided to ask this parent if she would be willing to teach me how to quilt. She immediately said, 'Of course, what kind of machine do you have?'

"I replied, 'I don't have one. I've never even touched a sewing machine before.' I am sure this parent, now my good friend, quilting buddy, and mentor thought to herself, 'Oh boy, what have I gotten myself into!'

"It has been two years now, and I have made so many quilts and gifted love and comfort to many. My first quilt, a Big Wonky Star, was for my 92-year-old grandmother who was always cold. Unfortunately, she passed away before I could finish. Thankfully, I did find someone else to gift the quilt to, and she began quilting as well!

"I absolutely love quilting. I watch Jenny all the time and I love making her quilts. I have made great friends and have shared my love for quilting with my other friends. We all love it! I still love watching and learning from Jenny. I watch the new tutorial every week on Friday for a new quilt pattern and great ideas. Thank you, Jenny and Missouri Star!"

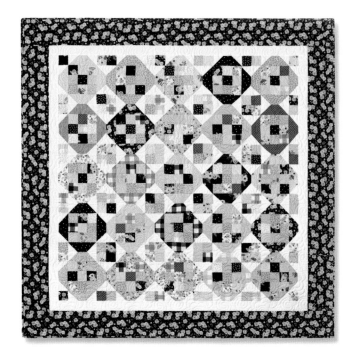

materials

QUILT SIZE
65" x 65"

BLOCK SIZE
10" finished

QUILT TOP
1 roll 2½" print strips
1 junior roll 2½" background strips*
  - includes inner border

OUTER BORDER
1¼ yards

BINDING
¾ yard

BACKING
4 yards - vertical seam(s)
  or 2 yards 108" wide

__Note:__ A junior roll contains 20 strips.

SAMPLE QUILT
Modern Farmhouse by Simple Simon
& Company for Riley Blake

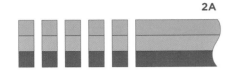

2A

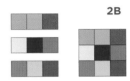

2B

3A

3B

3C

3D

1 cut

Select (25) print strips and cut (4) 2½" x 6½" rectangles and (4) 2½" squares from each strip. Set the rectangles, squares, and remaining print strips aside for the moment. Be sure to keep the matching rectangles together in sets of 4.

Cut 13 background strips into 2½" squares. Each background strip will yield (16) 2½" squares and **total of 200** are needed. Set the remaining strips aside for the inner border.

2 make 9-patches

Select 3 differing print strips. Sew them together lengthwise using ¼" seam allowances to make a strip set. Press all of the seam allowances in the same direction. **Make 5** strip sets.

Cut each strip set into 2½" increments to create 3-patch units. Each strip set will yield (16) 3-patch units and a **total of 75** are needed. **2A**

Select 3 differing 3-patch units. Nest the seams and sew them together to make a 9-patch unit as shown. **Make (25)** 9-patch units. **2B**

3 make snowballed rectangles

Mark a diagonal line corner to corner on the back of each 2½" background square. **3A**

Taking a 2½" x 6½" print rectangle cut earlier, lay a marked background square on either end as shown. **3B**

Sew along the marked line to snowball the 2 corners. Trim the excess fabric away leaving a ¼" seam allowance. **3C**

Open and press the seam allowances toward the center. **Make 100** snowballed rectangles. **3D**

Note: Be sure to continue organizing the rectangles in matching sets of 4.

4 block construction

Sew a snowballed rectangle to both sides of a 9-patch unit as shown. Press the seam allowances toward the rectangles. **Make 25. 4A**

Sew a 2½" print square to both ends of a snowballed rectangle. Press the seam allowances toward the center. **Make 50. 4B**

Lay out your block as shown. Nest the seams and sew the units together. **Make 25** blocks. **4C 4D**

Block Size: 10" finished

5 arrange & sew

Referring to the diagram on page 83, lay out your blocks in **5 rows** of **5 blocks** each. Sew the blocks together in rows. Press the seam allowances of all odd-numbered rows to the left and all even-numbered rows to the right. Nest the seams and sew the rows together.

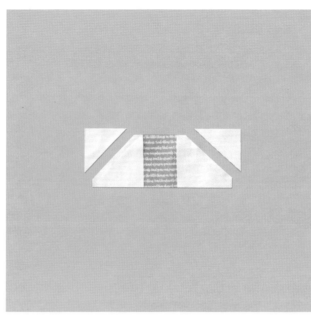

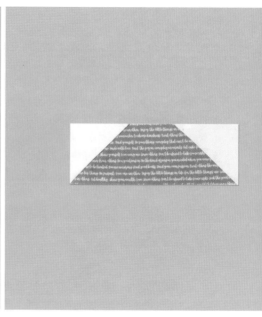

1 Select 3 differing 3-patch units. Nest the seams and sew them together to make a 9-patch unit as shown.

2 Lay a marked background square on either end of a 2½" x 6½" print rectangle as shown. Sew along the marked line to snowball the 2 corners. Trim the excess fabric away leaving a ¼" seam allowance.

3 Open and press the seam allowances toward the center. Make 4 snowballed rectangles.

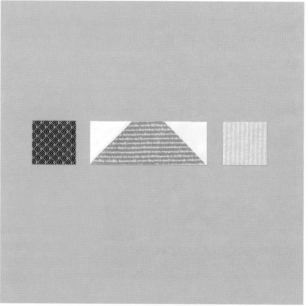

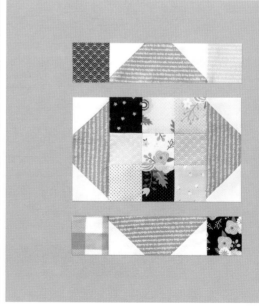

4 Sew a snowballed rectangle to both sides of a 9-patch unit as shown. Press the seam allowances toward the rectangles.

5 Sew a 2½" print square to both ends of a snowballed rectangle. Press the seam allowances toward the center. Make 2.

6 Lay out your block as shown. Nest the seams and sew the units together.

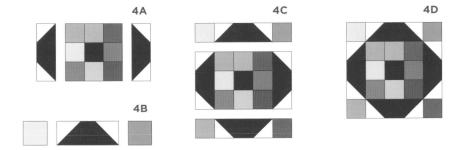

6 inner border

Pick up 6 of the 2½" background strips you set aside earlier and sew them end-to-end to make 1 long strip. Set the remaining strip aside for another project. Trim the borders from the long strip.

Refer to Borders (pg. 102) in the Construction Basics to measure and cut the inner borders. The strips are approximately 50½" for the sides and approximately 54½" for the top and bottom.

7 outer border

Cut (6) 6" strips across the width of the fabric. Sew the strips together end-to-end to make 1 long strip. Trim the borders from this strip.

Refer to Borders (pg. 102) in the Construction Basics to measure and cut the outer borders. The strips are approximately 54½" for the sides and approximately 65½" for the top and bottom.

8 quilt & bind

Layer the quilt with batting and backing and quilt. After the quilting is complete, square up the quilt and trim away all excess batting and backing. Add binding to complete the quilt. See Construction Basics (pg. 102) for binding instructions.

Just Looking
Turn Style Quilt

My name is Philip Cummings, I am a guy, and I am a quilter. Here is my story. It began 12 years ago. I had the day off, and I decided to go for a drive, nowhere in particular. A little back story, no one in my family is a quilter, not Mom's side, not Dad's side. So I didn't "get it" from anyone. I'd never heard of Bernina, Janome, Baby Lock, etc. And if you had asked me if I wanted to learn how to sew, not a chance. Okay, back to the story.

So, I am driving around and I see this strip mall, and having time on my hands, I decide to go explore. I pull into the parking lot and park and there is this shop on the end called "Susan Marie's Sewing Center." That's where it all started. So I say, "Okay, let's see what's in there." I go in and without noticing, probably got *the look*. The ladies asked if I needed any help and I said, "Just looking." Well, I proceeded to walk around this shop and there was a flannel quilt hanging in the corner that just hit me. My next thought was, *I gotta learn how to do that!* I continued to walk around and then I left.

Well, you would think that would be the end of it, right? Wrong. The next week I went back. I don't know why, but something deep down inside me was sparked. I continued to return to the shop in the weeks that followed, getting to know the sewing machines and the ladies, and finally, one of them asked me if I was ready to buy a machine. HUH? (Insert record scratch sound here). Me? Sew?

I asked what was the least expensive machine they had. After all, if it turned out I didn't like this, I was not going to be stuck with an expensive sewing machine. Two months after this story began, I have a sewing machine and I have NO IDEA what to do with it. The women at the shop showed me what a ¼" seam was and showed me how to thread the needle and off I went.

So, I decided to take a quilting class. In my previous visits to the shop, I saw how much fabric cost, and I thought, *there has to be less expensive fabric somewhere else.* Let's just say I learned the saying "you get what you pay for." I ended up re-buying all new fabric for my class that was good quality quilting fabric.

Jump ahead and I'm hooked. I ended up buying the Bernina 440 with embroidery. I have had two machine upgrades since then and I'm loving every minute of it!

What do I quilt? I have been commissioned to make two quilts, I've made a quilt or two for myself, and then I decided to make a quilt for my nieces' and nephews' firstborn babies.

I have been to Paducah, Kentucky, to the quilt museum and I have visited Missouri Star Quilt Co. at least three times, most recently for their 10th Birthday Bash.

Just last week, I was browsing and this lady came up to me and said, "I thought to myself, he's either a quilter or he's shopping for his wife, but I can't figure out which one it is." Do I love quilting? Yes! Do I still get *the look*? Yes! Do I mind? No!

materials

QUILT SIZE
85" x 85"

BLOCK SIZE
11½" finished

QUILT TOP
1 package 10" print squares
  - includes pieced border
1 package 10" background squares

PIECED BORDER
½ yard background fabric
  - matching background squares

OUTER BORDER
1½ yards

BINDING
¾ yard

BACKING
7¾ yards - vertical seam(s)
  or 2¾ yards of 108" wide

SAMPLE QUILT
Prose by Maywood Studio

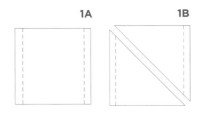

1A 1B

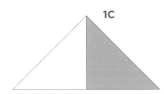

1C

1D

1E

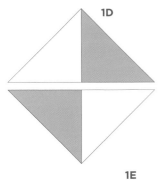

2A 2B

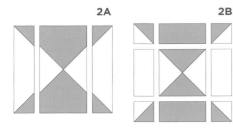

1 sew hourglass units

Select (36) 10″ print squares and (36) 10″ background squares and set the rest of the print and background squares aside for the pieced border.

Layer a background square on top of a print square with right sides facing. Sew down the right and left sides of the stacked squares using a ¼″ seam allowance. **1A**

Cut the sewn squares on 1 diagonal and open to reveal 2 pieced triangle units. Press the seams of each unit toward the darker fabric. **1B 1C**

Arrange the 2 pieced triangle units as shown. Nest the seams and sew them together to create an hourglass unit. **1D**

Square to 13″. Repeat the previous instructions to make a **total of 36** hourglass units. **1E**

2 block construction

Tip: You may find a rotating cutting mat or a small cutting mat you can pick up and turn helpful for cutting in multiple directions without disturbing the fabric.

Lay an hourglass unit on your cutting surface. Trim a 3″ pieced rectangle from both sides. **2A**

Without disturbing the fabric, trim 3″ across the top and bottom to create (4) 3″ half-square triangle units, (4) 3″ x 7″ rectangles and (1) 7″ hourglass unit. **2B**
Turn the center hourglass unit 90°. **2C**

Turn each of the corner half-square triangle units 180°. **2D**

Sew the block together in 3 rows as shown. Press the seam allowances of the top and bottom rows toward the center rectangle, and the seam allowances of the middle row

toward the outside rectangles. Nest the seams and sew the rows together to create the block. **Make 36. 2E**

Block Size: 11½″ finished

3 arrange & sew

Lay out the blocks in **6 rows** with each row being made of **6 blocks** making note of the orientation of the blocks in the diagram on page 89 as needed. Every other block is turned 90°, creating pinwheels where block corners meet. Sew the blocks together to form rows.

Press the seam allowances of the odd-numbered rows to the right and the seam allowances of the even-numbered rows to the left.

Nest the seams and sew the rows together to complete the quilt center.

4 pieced border

Pick up the 10″ print squares and background squares set aside earlier. Only 4 squares of each are needed for the pieced border, but you may wish to use all 6 print squares for more variation. Set any 10″ squares not chosen aside for another project.

Cut each 10″ square you chose in half horizontally and vertically. Each 10″ square will create (4) 5″ squares and a **total of 13** of both the print and the background 5″ squares are needed.

Layer a background square on top of a print square with right sides facing. Sew around all 4 sides of the stacked squares using a ¼″ seam allowance. **4A**

Cut the sewn squares on both diagonals and open to reveal 4 half-square triangle units. Press the seams of each unit toward the darker fabric. Repeat the instructions

1 Layer a background square on top of a print square with right sides facing. Sew down the right and left sides of the stacked squares using a ¼" seam allowance. Cut the sewn squares on a diagonal.

2 Open to reveal 2 pieced triangle units. Press the seams of each unit toward the darker fabric. Arrange the units as shown, nest the seams, and sew them together to create an hourglass unit.

3 Square the unit to 13".

4 Trim a 3" pieced rectangle from both sides. Without disturbing the fabric, trim 3" across the top and bottom to create (4) 3" half-square triangle units, (4) 3" x 7" rectangles and (1) 7" hourglass unit.

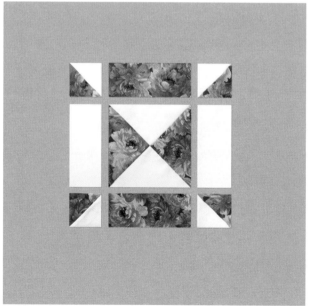

5 Turn the center hourglass unit 90°. Turn each of the corner half-square triangle units 180°.

6 Sew the block together in 3 rows as shown. Nest the seams and sew the rows together to create the block.

2C

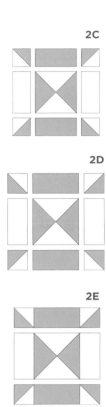

2D

2E

triangle units. Square each unit to 3″ and set them aside for the moment. **4B**

Cut (5) 3″ strips across the width of the background fabric. Subcut each strip into (5) 3″ x 7″ rectangles for a **total of (24)** 3″ x 7″ rectangles.

Refer to Borders (pg. 102) in the Construction Basics to measure the quilt center. The quilt center should be approximately 69½″ x 69½″.

Arrange 12 varying 3″ half-square triangle units and (6) 3″ x 7″ rectangles as shown. Sew the half-square triangle units and rectangles to create a pieced border, approximately 69½″ long. Adjustments can be made to the pieced border by taking in or letting out seams. **Make 4. 4C**

To create the top and bottom pieced borders, sew a half-square triangle to each end of 2 pieced borders as shown. The top and bottom pieced borders should be approximately 74½″ long. **4D**

Refer to the diagram below to lay out the pieced borders, paying close attention to the orientation of the borders. Sew a 69½″ pieced border to each side of the quilt center. Sew a 74½″ pieced border to the top and bottom of the quilt center.

5 outer border

Cut (8) 6″ strips across the width of the outer border fabric. Sew the strips together end-to-end to make 1 long strip. Trim the outer borders from this strip.

Refer to Borders (pg. 102) in the Construction Basics to measure and cut the outer borders. The strips are approximately 74½″ for the sides and 85½″ for the top and bottom.

6 quilt & bind

Layer the quilt with batting and backing and quilt. After the quilting is complete, square up the quilt and trim away all excess batting and backing. Add binding to complete the quilt. See Construction Basics (pg. 102) for binding instructions.

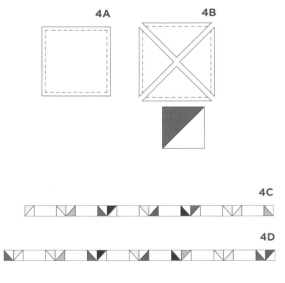

4A   **4B**

4C

4D

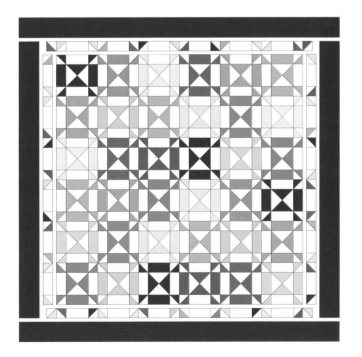

Reference

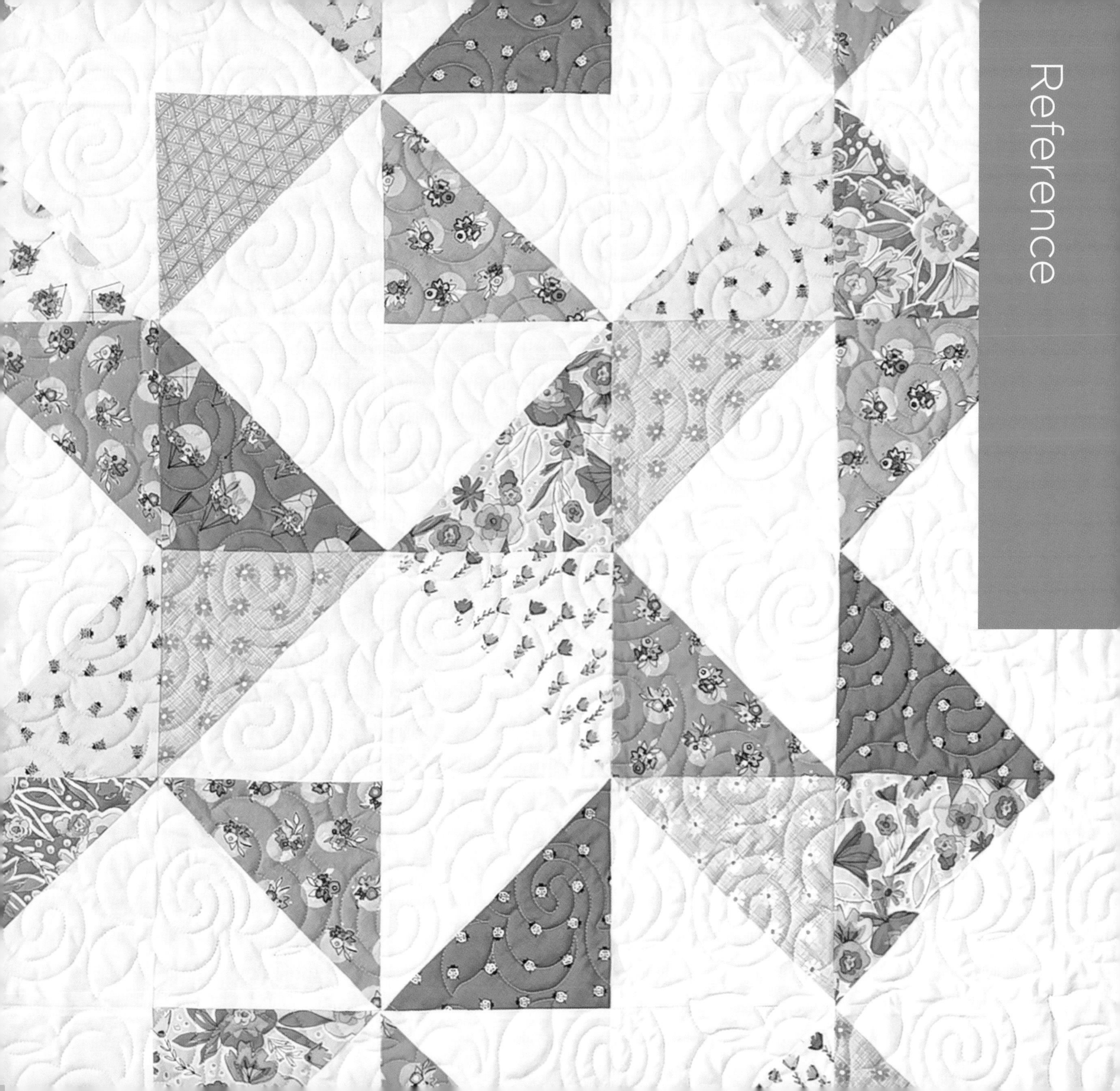

Around the Square Quilt

QUILT SIZE
78″ x 78″

BLOCK SIZE
7″ finished

QUILT TOP
1 package 10″ print squares*
1 package 10″ background squares

INNER BORDER
¾ yards
    - matching background squares

OUTER BORDER
1½ yards

BINDING
¾ yard

BACKING
4¾ yards - vertical seam(s)**
    or 2½ yards 108″ wide

OTHER
Missouri Star Quilt Company
    Small Simple Wedge Template

*__Note:__ You will need (41) 10″ print squares that contrast
your background fabric. If your package has some squares
that do not contrast, you'll need to replace those squares
with 10″ squares cut from a coordinating print fabric. Different
coordinating fabric can be used and up to (4) 10″ squares
can be cut from each ½ yard._

**__Note:__ Backing fabric must have 42″ of usable width._

SAMPLE QUILT
Cherry Lemonade by Jason Yenter
for In the Beginning Fabrics

QUILTING PATTERN
Champange Bubbles

PATTERN
P. 30

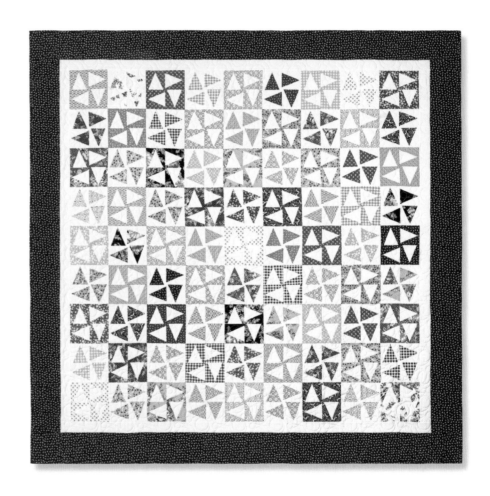

Calico Star Quilt

QUILT SIZE
91″ x 91″

BLOCK SIZE
24″ finished

QUILT TOP
1 package 10″ print squares
1 package 10″ background squares
1½ yards background fabric
   - includes inner border

OUTER BORDER
1¾ yards - includes cornerstones

BINDING
¾ yard

BACKING
8¼ yards - vertical seam(s)
   or 2¾ yards of 108″ wide

SAMPLE QUILT
Sun Print 2020 by Alison Glass
   for Andover

PATTERN
Feathering Meandering

PAGE
P. 14

Calico Star Pillow

PROJECT SIZE
Fits a 16″ pillow form

BLOCK SIZE
9″ finished

PROJECT SUPPLIES
(9) 5″ dark print squares
(9) 5″ light print squares
1 yard coordinating print
 - includes borders and pillow back
18″ square of batting

OPTIONAL PILLOW INSERT
½ yard muslin
Fiberfill

PATTERN
P. 21

Cottage Stars Table Runner

PROJECT SIZE
36" x 17"

BLOCK SIZES
4" x 5½" finished and 6" finished

PROJECT TOP
1 package 5" print squares
½ yard background fabric

BINDING
¼ yard

BACKING
¾ yard

SAMPLE QUILT
Painterly Petals by Studio RK for Robert Kaufman Fabrics

QUILTING PATTERN
Stars & Loops

PATTERN
P. 36

Happy Hearts
Quilt

QUILT SIZE
73″ x 73″

BLOCK SIZE
30″ finished

QUILT TOP
1 package 10″ print squares
1 package 10″ background squares

INNER BORDER
¾ yard

OUTER BORDER
1¼ yards

BINDING
¾ yard

BACKING
4½ yards - vertical seam(s)
  or 2¼ yards of 108″ wide

SAMPLE QUILT
Petals and Pots by Gabrielle Niel Design
Studio for Riley Blake Designs

QUILTING PATTERN
Curly Twirly Flowers

PATTERN
P. 24

Heart to Heart Table Runner

PROJECT SIZE
46" x 13"

BLOCK SIZE
9" finished

PROJECT TOP
1 package 5" print squares
2 coordinating 5"
   light print squares
   or ¼ yard of light print

BINDING
½ yard

BACKING
¾ yard - cut parallel to the
   selvages and sewn together
   along the short ends

SAMPLE QUILT
Bramble Cottage by Brenda Riddle
Designs for Moda Fabrics

QUILTING PATTERN
Hearts & Flowers

PATTERN
P. 74

Hopscotch
Quilt

QUILT SIZE
65" x 65"

BLOCK SIZE
10" finished

QUILT TOP
1 roll 2½" print strips
1 junior roll 2½" background strips*
  - includes inner border

OUTER BORDER
1¼ yards

BINDING
¾ yard

BACKING
4 yards - vertical seam(s)
  or 2 yards 108" wide

Note: *A junior roll contains 20 strips.*

SAMPLE QUILT
Modern Farmhouse by Simple
Simon & Company for Riley Blake

QUILTING PATTERN

PATTERN
P. 80

Summer Stars Quilt

QUILT SIZE
60" x 72"

BLOCK SIZES
11" finished and 6" finished

QUILT TOP
1 roll 2½" print strips
1 yard background fabric
   - includes inner border

OUTER BORDER
1½ yards

BINDING
¾ yard

BACKING
3¾ yards - horizontal seam(s)

OTHER
Clearly Perfect Slotted Trimmer - B

SAMPLE QUILT
Flour Garden by Linzee Kull
McCray for Moda Fabrics

QUILTING PATTERN
Variety

PATTERN
P. 46

Turn Style
Quilt

QUILT SIZE
85" x 85"

BLOCK SIZE
11½" finished

QUILT TOP
1 package 10" print squares
  - includes pieced border
1 package 10" background squares

PIECED BORDER
½ yard background fabric
  - matching background squares

OUTER BORDER
1½ yards

BINDING
¾ yard

BACKING
7¾ yards - vertical seam(s)
  or 2¾ yards of 108" wide

SAMPLE QUILT
Prose by Maywood Studio

QUILTING PATTERN
Paisley Feather

PATTERN
P. 84

Window Box Quilt

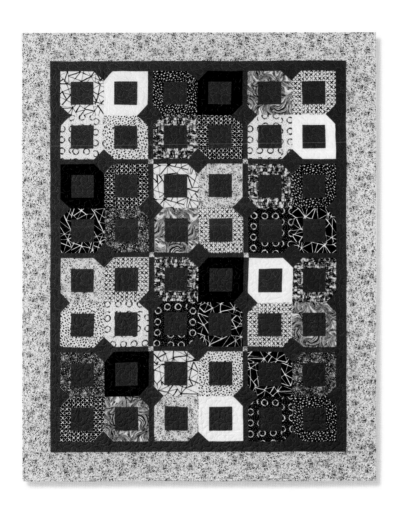

QUILT SIZE
68" x 86"

BLOCK SIZE
17" finished

QUILT TOP
1 roll 2½" print strips*
2¼ yards background fabric
  - includes sashing and inner
  border**

OUTER BORDER
1½ yards

BINDING
¾ yard

BACKING
5¼ yards - vertical seam(s)
  or 2¾ yards 108" wide

*Note: Your print strips must have at least 42"
of usable width and have at least 8 pairs of
matching strips.*

**Note: 2 packages of 5" background squares
and 1 yard of matching background fabric can
be substituted.*

SAMPLE QUILT
Pen and Ink by Studio RK for
Robert Kaufman Fabrics

Enchanted Kona Color of the Year
2020 by Robert Kaufman Fabrics

QUILTING PATTERN
Simple Stipple

PATTERN
P. 68

Construction Basics

General Quilting

- All seams are ¼" inch unless directions specify differently.
- Cutting instructions are given at the point when cutting is required.
- Precuts are not prewashed; therefore do not prewash other fabrics in the project.
- All strips are cut width of fabric.
- Remove all selvages.

Press Seams

- Use a steam iron on the cotton setting.
- Press the seam just as it was sewn right sides together. This "sets" the seam.
- With dark fabric on top, lift the dark fabric and press back.
- The seam allowance is pressed toward the dark side. Some patterns may direct otherwise for certain situations.
- Follow pressing arrows in the diagrams when indicated.
- Press toward borders. Pieced borders may demand otherwise.
- Press diagonal seams open on binding to reduce bulk.

Borders

- Always measure the quilt top 3 times before cutting borders.
- Start measuring about 4" in from each side and through the center vertically.
- Take the average of those 3 measurements.
- Cut 2 border strips to that size. Piece strips together if needed.
- Attach 1 to either side of the quilt.

- Position the border fabric on top as you sew. The feed dogs can act like rufflers. Having the border on top will prevent waviness and keep the quilt straight.
- Repeat this process for the top and bottom borders, measuring the width 3 times.
- Include the newly attached side borders in your measurements.
- Press toward the borders.

Binding

find a video tutorial at: www.msqc.co/006

- Use 2½" strips for binding.
- Sew strips end-to-end into one long strip with diagonal seams, aka the plus sign method (next). Press seams open.
- Fold in half lengthwise wrong sides together and press.
- The entire length should equal the outside dimension of the quilt plus 15" - 20."

Plus Sign Method

- Lay 1 strip across the other as if to make a plus sign right sides together.
- Sew from top inside to bottom outside corners crossing the intersections of fabric as you sew.
  Trim excess to ¼" seam allowance.
- Press seam open.

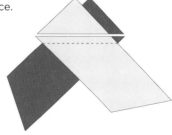

find a video tutorial at: www.msqc.co/001

Attach Binding

- Match raw edges of folded binding to the quilt top edge.
- Leave a 10″ tail at the beginning.
- Use a ¼″ seam allowance.
- Start in the middle of a long straight side.

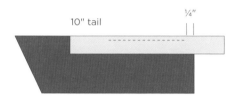

Miter Corners

- Stop sewing ¼″ before the corner.
- Move the quilt out from under the presser foot.
- Clip the threads.
- Flip the binding up at a 90° angle to the edge just sewn.
- Fold the binding down along the next side to be sewn, aligning raw edges.
- The fold will lie along the edge just completed.
- Begin sewing on the fold.

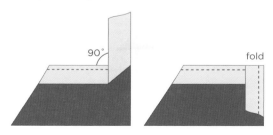

Close Binding

MSQC recommends The Binding Tool from TQM Products to finish binding perfectly every time.

- Stop sewing when you have 12″ left to reach the start.
- Where the binding tails come together, trim excess leaving only 2½″ of overlap.
- It helps to pin or clip the quilt together at the 2 points where the binding starts and stops. This takes the pressure off of the binding tails while you work.
- Use the plus sign method to sew the 2 binding ends together, except this time when making the plus sign, match the edges. Using a pencil, mark your sewing line because you won't be able to see where the corners intersect. Sew across.

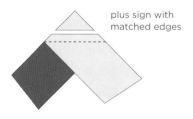

plus sign with matched edges

- Trim off excess; press seam open.
- Fold in half wrong sides together, and align all raw edges to the quilt top.
- Sew this last binding section to the quilt. Press.
- Turn the folded edge of the binding around to the back of the quilt and tack into place with an invisible stitch or machine stitch if you wish.